When You Just Can't *Say Good-bye,* Don't

A Mother's Personal Journey After Losing a Child

To Carla,
With my deep thanks for your support—
Wishing you rainbows always!
Maria Malin

MARIA MALIN

ISBN: 1-4392-3214-8
ISBN-13: 9781439232149

Visit www.booksurge.com to order additional copies.

This book is dedicated with all my love

to my children,

Francesca, Steven, Jr. and Brianna,

my three greatest gifts from God.

~ Always three they will be ~

To my husband Steve,

my friend, my love, my life…

We have walked through this storm together,

and chosen to look for the rainbows on the other side.

Thank you, precious family,

for giving me the time I needed

to turn our story into this book.

To personally acknowledge the hundreds of people we are so blessed to have in our lives, who have influenced the meaning behind this book, and who continue to walk this path with our family, would take hundreds of pages alone.

To all of you,
know that we will never forget each thoughtful word and deed,
your strength, your prayers, your presence
kept the light burning through this dark tunnel.

Thank you and God bless you.

TABLE OF CONTENTS

Part III: Living in Our New World

FOREWORD

There is no greater good-bye to say than when your child dies. No greater loss, no greater separation. I guess I'm not very good at the world's worst good-bye. I know I couldn't say it to my own child.

Indeed, my safe world completely changed on April 19, 2003, when my eleven year-old son, Steven, was killed in an accident. Through this life-changing experience, I have learned that there are a thousand ways to say good-bye to a loved one. Wakes and funerals, for starters, create quite the send-off. Did I mention that I hate wakes and funerals? Grief books and bereavement support bring solace, comfort. I didn't want to bring comfort to death. I wanted death to go away. I don't remember inviting death to knock at our door, and I certainly didn't want to answer that knock. I wondered if there was *another way*. I wondered if you could truly defy everything that death represents. Separation. Loss. Pain. Sadness.

When You Just Can't Say Good-bye, Don't is the alternative to every parent's most impossible good-bye. It is the story of how to keep the hello's coming, how to fight to keep the precious loved one you've physically lost close to every remaining day of your own life. It is the story to read when you want "hope" instead of "hopeless." You will find "life" again, with healthy ways to move forward and hang on.

> *". . . we fix our eyes not on what is seen, but on what is unseen.*
> *For what is seen is temporary, but what is unseen is eternal."*
> *2 Corinthians 4:18*

* * *

CHAPTER 1: THE BIGGEST "NO" OF OUR LIVES

I've never been very good at taking "no" for an answer. I believe in the "negotiability" factor in life. You know, "let's talk this through and see if we can come up with a solution that'll make everyone happy." Compromise. Counter-offer. Negotiate, negotiate, negotiate. When I was young, I didn't believe in luck. I believed in working hard, being ready for opportunities, and always striving for what you want. Making the teams, getting the grades, earning the honors. You just approach any situation with the right "approach," and then "no" is not an option.

Until your child dies. The absolute biggest, unfathomable, unmistakable "no" you will ever hear is that your child has died. Talk about a zero proposition. No counter offer there. There's no negotiating someone telling you that you will never, ever again hold, kiss, comfort, care for, or physically be with your child, teach them to drive, watch them graduate, attend their wedding, baby-sit the grandchildren they give you. Indeed, in one fell swoop, someone breaks the news that your life, as you know it, is over. Really, truly over. End of deal. And you're supposed to accept this?

On Saturday, April 19, 2003, the day before Easter, my 11 year-old son, Steven Brian Malin, Jr., middle brother to 14 year-old Francesca, and almost 9 year-old Brianna, cherished namesake to my husband, Steve, honor student, math wiz, baseball catcher, basketball player, altar server and violinist, celebrated the end of Lent at 12:00 noon by walking down the street with one of his best friends, a dear, blond-haired little boy named Garrett Paffenroth, to the local McDonald's where we live in Lake Forest, Illinois — a small, upscale suburb on the North Shore of Lake Michigan, about thirty miles from Chicago. For forty days, Steven had given up soda for his Lenten sacrifice, through a bout of the stomach flu when ginger ale would have really hit the spot, through a spring break trip to Marco Island, Florida, when dining out every night included pop for all, except him. So, on Holy Saturday, with no regular sports scheduled for the holiday weekend, I decided to reward Steven with a walk to McDonald's a block down from our house to celebrate with his first pop in forty days. And a six-piece chicken nugget Happy Meal. A quick lunch with a good buddy followed by a game of catch at the park directly across the street from our house and home by 3:00 to color Easter eggs. Sounded like a plan.

Until on the walk home, my only son, my beloved Steven got hit by a freight train which was crossing paths with a commuter train that had come into our nearby train station for a stop.

He was hit from behind, pummeled into a brick wall that lined the train station walkway, thrown mid-air and slammed into his death.

My husband and I arrived within minutes of Steven's arrival at the emergency room, a team still giving him CPR. Outside his room, a kindly, stoic head nurse with blond hair and a blank expression and a portly, gentle-faced older emergency room doctor first talked with us before we were allowed to see him. We were brought into the "family room," which we now know as the room they take you to when the news is very, very grim. As they spoke, I felt like I was listening to voices in exaggerated slow motion. "He has no active vital signs at this moment. He is on a machine to monitor any heart activity and we are receiving none. He has been receiving CPR since the first paramedic arrived at the scene of the accident, but was without oxygen for several minutes. We know he has a broken neck and numerous internal injuries." The news could not have been worse. My husband and I looked at each other, suddenly snapping back into "flight or fight" mode, and begged to get in there immediately and see him firsthand. The doctor and nurse looked at each other and must have figured that we needed to see Steven ourselves to come to the conclusion they were so delicately trying to point out — that Steven had not survived being hit by the freight train. In our state of shock, nothing was registering. In my own exploding mind, I just needed to get in there to take over. In that instant of adrenaline rush, I truly believed that once I got in the room with Steven, all would be fixed. After all, isn't that what a mother is for? These people, competent though they seemed, did not carry Steven for nine months, give birth to all 8 pounds, 7 ounces and twenty and a half inches of him, know every nuance of his health, his needs, his being on this earth. Only a mom could tackle a situation as serious as this. And God help me, I was ready for the fight of my life.

My husband and I ran into the room where Steven lay unmoving. He had a brace around his neck and was flat on his back. I think I shoved everyone but the administer of CPR out of the way and began to plead with Steven to fight. I screamed, "Fight, fight! Come on, one breath is all I need, sweetie. You do it for Mom. Come on now; please try for me, Steven. For Mom. PLEASE, STEVEN. You can do it. One breath for Mom. You can't leave us! Please, dear Lord, please. God, no, no, no!!!" I opened his lids, and beneath the long, fringed black lashes and into the soft, soft brown of his eyes, I saw fixed pupils. I searched his body for signs of injury, and basically saw that his body was severely and completely crushed by the impact of the train throwing him into the wall, every bone in his body appearing broken. Ironically, the only mark on his beautiful face was the slight scratch he got diving for quarters in the pool in Florida just two weeks before. I hugged him and kissed his face and cold hands and chest where the paddles made indelible red marks on his spring break Florida-tanned skin. His head was gashed open from behind and bled incessantly, the bandages being changed every few minutes. And still I begged and controlled what I thought was a reversible situation and fought for my Steven with every ounce of my strength, hoping I could infuse my motherly magic into these hopeless moments and change the outcome.

The moments in that emergency room ticked into minutes, and the minutes slowly turned into fifteen. The looks around the room, with no sign of life from our son, gave way to the inevitable acknowledgement that he had not survived, that it was time to remove the CPR and let him go. *Let him go?* It was purely, plainly unconscionable to me. I stood there furious and confused and feeling like I would hyperventilate, my husband vomiting over the scrub sink and being assisted by a nurse in his own shock. The head nurse grabbed me by the arm and whispered, "You have to let him go. He's gone now." *Let him go?* Are you crazy? Let my only son, my little buddy, my sweet, smart, funny Steven *go*? NEVER!!!!!

At exactly 2:00 p.m., Steven was formally pronounced dead. We were pronounced "dead" at that moment as well. There is nothing in this entire cruel world more punishing, more severely physically, emotionally and mentally punishing than to be told that your child has died. And with that news, we heard the biggest "no" of our lives.

* * *

CHAPTER 2: A DIFFERENT "YES"

Maya Angelou writes, "I've learned that people will forget what you said, will forget what you did, but people will never forget how you made them feel." My purpose in writing this book is to help you feel hope when you have been given the most hopeless news imaginable, the biggest "no" of your life. I wish to help you continue to feel the bond, the connection, the magic of your loved one, be it a child, spouse, parent, grandparent, friend. To tell you that the last thing you need to do or should do is *let go*.

If you have gone through the loss of a child, you have undoubtedly already heard the well-meaning comments from well-meaning friends and family who tell you that you will survive, go on with your life, and *get over* this loss one day. I vehemently disagree with this advice. Instead, I am a strong proponent of *hanging on*. As in, don't let go for a minute. Keep that child close to every remaining day of your life, every breath you take. Restructure your life to incorporate a new relationship with that child, a different type of parenting of that child's memory, *recognizing the signs and symbols* that your child is still close — realizing that if you believe, you will receive.

My child's strengths, weaknesses, pastimes and passions left an indelible imprint of symbols in my world, which to me represent all things "Steven." Although he's no longer physically here, he's left a powerful trail of signs for me in my daily life. Everywhere I turn, I see something that reminds me of this loving little boy. I look for these symbols, and sometimes they simply come to me. I strongly believe that our loved ones send "signs" to us that they are near, truly just around the corner or over our shoulder. My entire family has had numerous signs from Steven. I know that the signs come to all of us because we have chosen not to sever the relationship with our son, brother, grandson, nephew, cousin, buddy, teammate. Because we have chosen to not say good-bye, he has not, either. His physical body may be no more, but his spiritual energy is everywhere in our daily world.

I have read so many, too many grief books about the journey alone. I have learned too many ways to get past death. I disagree with just about all of them. I don't want to feel victorious because I got "beyond" death and mourning. I will always feel death when I visit Steven's mausoleum. How can you not when there are hundreds of dead all around you? I want to frequent places that remind me of him alive and enjoying his life. I want to focus on life itself. Most grief books have left me with more sadness, more grief feelings, more death. I wanted "life" back.

So this is my personal story. No interviews. No research. My journey if you want to walk my way. My path if you want to share it. I didn't want to go it alone without Steven. I wanted to continue my life's journey with him on it. You can come along, too.

I will help you find healthy, well-adjusted ways to continue to honor your child in your home, your hearts, and for the ultimate benefit of the rest of your family. I am not an advocate of candles and shrines. I won't tell you to transform your child into some saint or angel to pray to or worship. Steven was a regular boy who lived a regular life. This is what we celebrate. These are the stories that still bring us laughter when Steven's name enters our family's daily conversation.

I know what it's like to be asked how many children you have and want to collapse. I know how scary it is to step back out into a world that you think you don't know anymore because it's robbed you of "life" as you knew it. I wish to walk those first steps with you, help you climb stairs again, and get to a place where you're living life with new meaning, not just running away from death. I want to teach you how to infuse the spirit of your precious child into every holiday season, birthday and anniversary that you'll celebrate for the rest of your own life. (That's right, I said "celebrate.") Even everyday errands and family outings can include your child if you let them.

You will have to make a conscious, determined effort to accomplish this momentous task. But if you are up for the challenge of your lifetime, if you are truly, honestly ready to keep your loved one with you and not allow death to take them away, read the rest of the pages of this book, and don't take "no" for an answer. Why spend the rest of your life in bleak darkness when you can still have light and hope? Why grieve alone when you and your family can do so much to keep life "full of life," not death?

You can't have the rainbow without the rain; so first, let the rain fall. It fell hard for us, and if you are reading my book and have experienced significant loss, I know it has for you, too. I will not pretend for one second that the rain does not still come. That I don't still face some mornings and pray that I have just woken up from the worst possible nightmare ever. That this is all some big, bad mistake. Yet with the rain, I now choose to see the rainbows as well. In fact, my family seeks them out.

I have taken my time, over five years as of this writing, to just "feel." To put my thoughts and emotions down on paper just as I was feeling them. And with no one to judge me on what I was privately thinking or going through, I can now look back with a new perspective, with a will to go on and a willingness to share my feelings and hopefully help someone else who cannot say good-bye, either.

For the purpose of telling a complete story, I must begin with the obvious. I must share the painful journey of how I got to this point and how God, my family and friends gave me the strength to change the rest of this story back in my favor. I certainly didn't have a bolt of lightning strike and show me how to live with my son still by my side, with his spirit guiding my actions. You will read about all the ways in which we have chosen to reconfigure our lives, then discern, reflect and figure out what works for you. Our path will not be your exact path, but follow our story and see what's possible. It is my goal to show you a new way to live with grief, but still *live.* To take your biggest "no" and turn it into the "yes" that will lead the rest of your days with strength and resolve, keeping your child or loved one close to you. For me, there is no other way but to hang on. I hope you will, too.

Early on in my grief, I had to make a conscious decision. A decision to live. Not just to survive, but truly live again. Before Steven was taken away, I took a big bite out of life, and packed my days with purpose. I lived with goals, dreams and direction. After he was killed, I felt like all of my dreams, many of which included him, had been stripped from me in one horrendous strike. I could not make any sense or find any reason to explain why this had happened to my family. I initially thought that I would spend the rest of my days on this earth maybe surviving, maybe not. I would sit wondering what I did to deserve this, how I could've slighted God to such a degree to receive this highest punishment.

Then one day, I came to a crossroads, one which made me choose. And I chose life. Life that included Steven still with us. Of course, Steven will not achieve the milestones that his earthly life had promised. I will never see his adult life with marriage and children. Hey, I never even saw him graduate eighth grade. But I promise that if you have the courage to walk this journey with me, you will be okay. Your spouse will benefit. Your other children, if you have any, will grow up with their sibling by their side as well. To me, this is so vitally important to the future of everyone's well-being. I write from the pen of a mother who's lost a child, but I believe that no matter whom we've given up to death, we must still love them and preserve their place within us just as we did while they were living. To think differently from this view, to cut the ties completely, to sever the relationship of what was once one of, if not the most important relationship in your life is purely unthinkable to me. I pray that it is for you, too.

So, if you're trying to let go, shut this book. Don't waste one more minute of your time reading my philosophy. Because I choose to hang on. To have it all. To never take "no" for an answer when you can hear a joyous "yes." For me, to preserve and protect what is surely life's most precious gift. My child.

The rainbows will come if you choose to align your path to mine, of this I promise. They will color your life with new and different hues, but you will come to recognize the meaning of the colors. But again, you can't have the rainbow without the rain. So first, join me in the blackest, hail-pummeling hell you can imagine. The world says it over and over, and I now firmly agree. There is no greater pain than losing a child. But walk on with me past the storm. I'll show you rainbows. New colors. A new path. Light to guide this endless journey. Signs. Symbols. Promise. Hope. A *yes.*

* * *

PART I: FIRST THE STORM

CHAPTER 3: THE DARKEST HOURS

I didn't think anything could rival the horror of the emergency room — until we returned home to our other kids. Having been driven home by one of our dear priests and friends from St. Patrick's church in Lake Forest, Fr. Larry Hennessy, who had come to be with us at the hospital, we were met at the front door by our two daughters, Francesca and Brianna. I will never, never, never forget the confused, tear-streaked, hysterical looks on the girls' faces, so needing us to come in the door and tell them that this was all the biggest mistake imaginable, that the brother sandwiched between the two of them, whether on the couch, in a Christmas card picture or in the back seat of our SUV, was okay. Francesca was especially overwrought, so we tried to bring the kids to a more private place to talk, while the house was filling up with family members. My parents had come from their home across town already, as had a few of our siblings. One of my older brothers, Gene, had rushed over to our house to be with the girls. One of Steve's brothers, Randy, and his wife JoAnne, had met us at the hospital and followed back to the house. I had called my dear girlfriend, Sophia Childs, from the hospital to come and be with the girls until we got back. Although my mom was there, she was surely in a state of shock herself, and I didn't know if she could handle the emotional devastation that our daughters were going through while we were still with Steven. I knew Sophia could come and be the "mom strength" I needed her to be for my girls. Our other siblings would soon join in at the house; my only sister, Diane, and her family trying to get on a flight home from their spring break trip to Florida, and my other brother, Chris, at home with a horrible case of bronchitis. All of our immediate siblings lived in the Chicago area, and one by one, they ran, sped, and flew to our side as fast as their legs would carry them.

I wanted to be in control, and had always prided myself on taking control of situations. In these moments, returning to the home I shared with my family, seeing the pain of my daughters and knowing there was nothing I could do to reverse it, I have never, ever felt more out of control in my entire life. *No, my sweet girls, Steven is never coming back. No, this is not a mistake. God, where are you right now? My daughters need you to bring their brother back this instant!!!* Chaos was building everywhere, with everyone in extreme shock and no immediate opportunities for privacy or quiet. I alternated between screams, pleas and whimpers, feeling like I was upstairs, standing on some crumbling balcony, looking down at the worst emotional carnage of everyone I loved in life. But I wasn't on any balcony. I was down there with my loved ones, feeling repeatedly kicked in my stomach, stabbed in the heart, my flesh being torn away from my body. I heard myself repeatedly screaming, "Please God, NO, NO, NO! Please not Steven!!!" but I felt certain in those moments of horror that God didn't hear me. We also were victim to the intermittent, deafening blare of train horns themselves as they passed the freight train still parked at the scene of the accident, just down the street from our house. If only that horn had sounded in time to warn my little boy. The shrill noise combined with the devastation of those in our home combined to make the nightmare of the situation that much more unbearable.

I regret that I had no physical ability to comfort my girls. My sweet "Frankie," as Francesca had been nicknamed at birth by my husband, sobbed and sobbed. I had no means to calm her down. I felt like the worst mother in those moments. I was in such a blur myself that I couldn't focus on her needs. I had no words to take back the most horrific moments of her life. *Please, sweet Frankie, please stop crying.* My younger daughter Brianna, "Bri," (bree) as we all had come to call her, was so terribly confused. She barely spoke. I had no idea what was going through her head. Was she just in complete shock? Was she too young to absorb this ultimate tragedy? I eventually lost track of the girls in the house, Frankie's 8th grade friends quickly arriving, forming a protective circle around her in her bedroom; Bri being taken by family friends to get her out of the direct impact of the nightmare that continued to unfold. I had no idea what state they were in; I just knew that others were helping them in their immediate needs because I was completely, utterly useless to them.

The doorbell and phone rang constantly, a few of Steven's friends simply leaving voice mails for him to come out and play, not even aware yet that their buddy had just been killed and would never again be free to play catch or Nintendo. Our home continued to be bombarded with visitors, friends, and family, in shock and needing to see firsthand if this could possibly be true. As each entered, I wanted them to tell us that Steven was fine. Somebody had to have the news I needed to hear. *God, where are you??? I need you!* The news media even tried to find their way into our home, hoping to get that few minutes of coverage for the 10 o'clock news about the boy that was killed by a train that day. We felt attacked by demons, undercover reporters, train horns, the Grim Reaper himself laughing at us from that imaginary balcony. At one point, I stormed up to Steven's bedroom, thinking I'd find him there in my state of delirium, and only found baseball cards strewn all over his carpeting, his windows all open, and an unfamiliar breeze sending movement into a now lifeless room. *Steven, where are you??? I need you!* With Steven not at home, suddenly this did not feel like "home." We were prisoners in a jail of mass chaos and surreal horror.

Hour after hour, more visitors arrived and left, food appearing on trays from friends, train horns blaring for hours on end until the train that struck Steven was released to continue on its route. We would soon learn that other trains passing a stalled train, which had been in a deadly accident, sounded their horns in acknowledgement of the incident. *Yeah, where were the horns when we needed them???*

I relived each minute of that day over and over; Steven watching me make stuffed manicotti that morning for Easter dinner the next day, him joking with me about who he might marry someday who could cook his favorite Italian dishes, leaving Steven in the garage around noon to clean up his baseball equipment as I pulled away to pick up a few more things at the grocery store, a quick kiss on the cheek for the $10 I gave him and his friend to have their celebratory lunch at McDonald's, never to see him alive again, racing to a hospital where he lay on an emergency room table receiving CPR in vain, the exact minute he was officially pronounced dead. I remember screaming, "God, I'm so sorry for whatever I've done. Please bring Steven back!" Instead of accepting the condolences of all who arrived at our door; neighbors, community friends, my childhood friend Raphaela Davis who had just arrived back from a vacation with her husband Kirk, my dear girlfriend Georgianna Rossi who quietly held my hand, my oldest childhood friend Maria Kariotis who was frantically calling, trying to get back from a Disney cruise, her family's spring break trip, Jenny Zinser, Robin DiTomasso, Wendy and Frank Karkazis, good friends who simply rushed over to comfort us. So, so, many immediately there for us, but no one able to tell me that this didn't really happen. I finally succumbed to the mayhem, and stared blankly ahead between sobs and screams, my brother Gene's arm protectively over my shoulder in our study, ticking away the minutes of the end of my own life that afternoon.

Steve sat in the kitchen with his family, fixed and confused, so beyond distraught. Another of his brothers, David, had soon arrived with his wife Aggie, Randy still with us, all of them trying so hard to comfort their brother so lost in pain, so physically sick, still occasionally vomiting from shock. Our boy lay crushed on an emergency room table, and my poor, broken, empty husband sat crushed, annihilated from holding his only son dead in his arms just hours before.

We stayed up until very late into the night, partly to wait up for my sister, Diane, and her family, to arrive back from Florida, partly because no one had the courage to try to go to bed, Steve's brother Randy and his wife, Joanne, staying until around 1 or 2:00 in the morning. When we finally walked Brianna upstairs to get into her pajamas, she innocently asked if the Easter Bunny would still be visiting the next morning. "Oh, my dear baby. Of course, he will." It was a moment of reality squeezed in between hours of impossibility. I shook my head at the thought of this eight year-old's unencumbered question and realized that we had gotten a few special gifts for Steven that he'd been wanting for months, and had already forgotten that this was the night before Easter. Strange how quickly life as it should happen gets stripped away, and something as joyful as the Easter Bunny visiting becomes foreign. After Bri laid down, my husband and I decided to quickly put out the gifts we had gotten the kids, complete with the baskets, even for Steven. We could never have laid out only two baskets; it had to be three. As I looked down at a Purdue t-shirt and basketball shorts we had gotten him, a gift he had wanted for months, I wished with all my heart that I had given it to him the night before. He would never know that his Easter wish had come true. Putting the gifts out despite our complete disinterest in the holiday was solely based on bringing some small measure of comfort to our girls. Of course, no one would be celebrating anything the next day.

Back upstairs with the kids, they were afraid and unable to fall asleep, all of us soon congregating in our room, scared and exhausted but unable to possibly think about rest. I had been forced to take the only tranquilizer I would ever take in this mess, and it only served to make me feel extremely dizzy and out of control for several hours, anything but sleepy. Weeks later, I would be told by my internist that she could help me get "through" this situation or simply "around it" with medication, and I can now honestly say that I'm glad I chose to go through the fire, head-on. For me, sedatives would only temporarily mask what would inevitably need to happen, that being the true grief process, the complete feelings of devastation, my real descent to hell. I not only wanted to feel every emotion, I was also responsible for being coherent enough to help my other children, physically and emotionally. I couldn't leave them alone as I did that first day. I don't regret my decision to refuse tranquilizers, but would never judge someone who needs them to get through their shock. For me, it was important to look back and know that the pummeling I took was real, and every reaction was me, good, bad or otherwise. I was never numb. I felt every punch, stab, and kick to my guts, again and again. You wanna talk real? Unfortunately, it was real from that first call, and continues to be, every day of our lives.

On Easter morning, we took a few moments of respite before heading to the funeral home to let the kids open their small gifts and candy, and it was actually our first comfort to listen to Brianna explain how nice it was for the Easter Bunny to visit Steven even though he was in heaven now. From the first day, Bri knew that Steven was with God. We were the ones who questioned God's whereabouts for a long time. We told Brianna that she could have Steven's candy since he had special candy with God this Easter, although we hardly believed what we were saying. The girls would attend Easter Mass with Randy and Joanne as my husband and I, along with a few of our siblings, would head to the funeral home to make Steven's arrangements. No baked manicotti today, no Easter egg hunt, no family over for a pastel-colored holiday. We faced the worst morning imaginable for a parent; picking out your child's casket, writing their obituary, and planning the day for their wake and funeral. What do you write about your child's life, dreams and accomplishments when they've barely had a chance to live? Steven was a gentle boy, the best son and brother anyone could ask for, a true and loyal friend and teammate, good at sports, a kid who loved to make others laugh, with a true and healthy balance of focus and fun to his personality, and was even chosen to serve with the bishop at his sister's 8th grade Confirmation in a few days, ironically what would now be the day of his own funeral. Other than that, he barely made his mark. He was only eleven and a quarter years old.

After our return from the funeral home, our house was again filled with loved ones who kept their protective shield and constant hugs around all of us. No, we didn't celebrate Easter. And we continued to operate in a trance-like state, but we were never alone. We were blessed by our immediate families and dearest friends who saw to every detail of what would surely be the most grueling days of our lives just ahead of us.

* * *

CHAPTER 4: PLANNING THE GOOD-BYES

Steven's wake would take place on Tuesday evening, his funeral the following morning; again, tragically the day of Francesca's 8th grade Confirmation. Steven would have been so proud to be altar server for the bishop that night, participating in this important rite of passage for his big sister. Instead, we would be watching his casket carried down the very aisle in which Francesca would meet the bishop, unbelievably saying good-bye to Steven's chance to be confirmed, to graduate 8th grade himself, to live another seventy years or so of life. In two short days, one child of ours was due to confirm her Catholic faith as a young adult. Another child would never see his young adulthood.

On Monday morning, we decided to begin assembling the photo montages which would grace the funeral home, today's tradition of displaying the life of your loved one for all who come to say good-bye. We needed supplies, poster boards, etc., and I decided to head out to Office Max with Sophia, the same dear friend who had stayed with our children since the first frightening moments on Saturday. Before I left the house, I had a phone conversation with the principal of Steven's school, Mr. Kyle Schumacher, who had been telling me how difficult a time the 5th graders were having that morning, that the grief counselors couldn't seem to help, and that the children were really suffering. Knowing that we had to meet with our pastor, Fr. Bill McNulty, later that afternoon to plan the funeral, I asked our principal if it was okay to stop by the school afterwards to talk to the kids ourselves. I knew that they must be in such deep shock that it might help to connect with us in some way before the wake and funeral. I had also been told that the kids were scared of what might have happened to Steven's body from the accident, and whether it would be safe for them to view him at the wake.

On the way to Office Max to pick up the poster board for the photo collage, I had a spontaneous idea. When kids feel helpless, they need to help. I thought it might be a good idea to give them a little job in all of this so that they could feel like they were helping us out. I bought some extra supplies at the store, and would bring them to the school later that day. I found that focusing on others' pain in this nightmare, that of his innocent classmates, lessened my pain for a few moments as well.

Our immediate family and friends were busy sorting through photo albums at our house, also helping us with everything from making sure our girls were fed, that they had picked out clothes to wear for the services, and seeing to any and all other details we certainly were missing. Steve and I went on to the meeting with Fr. McNulty, and actually found laughter intermixed with many tears in preparing Steven's funeral Mass. Steven, Jr. was a wonderful blend of drive and achievement, humor and antics, with love and affection wrapping it all into one special little boy who gave the best "smasher" hugs ever. In reminiscing about the many funny stories featuring this ever-lively son of ours, we couldn't help but laugh through our tears, the bitter reality that Steven would never make us laugh again leveraged by the numerous times he had made those around him, especially his family and closest friends, hold their stomachs and roar. We chose favorite church music and mixed it up with Steven's favorite Jackson Five oldie, "I'll Be There." *You and I must make a pact. We must bring salvation back. Where there is love, I'll be there. I'll reach out my hand to you. I'll have faith in all you do. Just call my name and I'll be there.* A violinist, hired by Steven's old violin instructor, Mrs. Rosemary Schneider, would play his favorite piece entitled, "Starlight Waltz." We would include his many friends in the Catholic service, asking them to come up to the altar during the Rite of Peace and then go out to the congregation, beginning the Sign of Peace at each pew. We would have Steven's cousins bring up the offertory gifts and ask Garrett, Steven's great buddy who was with him at the accident, to be altar server. The four of us would all eulogize

Steven, but our brother-in-law Vince would read Francesca's words for her since she was too shy to get up at the lectern to say the good-byes herself. "*Dear Steven, Thank you so much for everything you did for me. You taught me most of all how not to be shy. If you didn't bless me you're your gift of being more outgoing, I would never know how to have fun with friends. God blessed us with your great smile. I remember just last Sunday when we told Brianna that we could read each other's minds and she believed us, for I only wish it were true. I love you so much, and I know that you are a guardian angel on all of our shoulders. I know that if you wanted anyone with you, it would be your best friends Bobby and Garrett. I love you so much. I am sorry I never got to say good-bye, but now I have. I love you, Francesca.*" Little Brianna would pen her sentiments to Steven as well, and read them aloud in front of the congregation. "*My brother was a loving, caring brother to me. He taught me how to do every naughty thing I know. My brother always kept my family happy. That's what I love about my loving brother. Also, he was always there for me. I loved my brother so much because he was the one who 'standed' beside me always. Love, Brianna.*" My dear girlfriends, Jenny Zinser, Peggy Schweller, Lisa Oberheide, Maria Kariotis, Robin DiTomasso, Raphaela Davis, and again, Sophia Childs, would assemble as a group at the lectern, taking turns sharing brief sentiments about Steven, speaking of his smasher hugs, his love of cheering his friends on in their sports, his patience and attention to the younger siblings of the group of families who were all such close friends. My sister Diane would offer a beautiful poem she wrote about Steven, and it read in part: "*Why? So many, many times this question has been raised, by all those touched and saddened these recent days. Why did it have to be a sunny, spring day? Why didn't Steven walk a different way?*" All in all, it would be a Mass that I know would have pleased Steven, not only because it included many people he loved so dearly, but because much effort went into the messages, the heartfelt and touching stories of his brief but important life. We also chose music that meant something to us. We would process into the church to "Jesus, Remember Me" and listen to "Amazing Grace" during Holy Communion. I had a favorite song called "You Are Mine" which I also asked the gifted vocalist from our church, Mrs. Dawn Isaia, to sing for Steven. The words to this hymn speak of Jesus bringing us all home to heaven, and although I still enjoy hearing it occasionally sung at Mass, the words now haunt me as I know that Steven has gone home to be with God, and I was anything but ready for him to leave on this journey. *"Do not be afraid, I am with you. I have called you each by name. Come and follow me. I will bring you home. I love you and you are mine."*

With all the preparations in place for Steven's funeral service, I felt a strange sense of calm when we left our priest. Looking back, I think that this temporary calm was preparing me for the next stop that afternoon, to Steven's school and his classroom.

My legs felt heavy as I walked into Deer Path Middle School in Lake Forest, having just been there to pick up Steven a few days ago, now entering as the mother of the same little boy who lay in a funeral home awaiting his final good-byes. My husband and I neared the door to Steven's classroom, which was filled with the noise of the fellow students from his team. A hush fell over the group as we entered, and we immediately saw the tired, teary strain on dozens of faces, dear children who needed to be comforted through this most extreme loss of one of their own. I considered walking right back out the door because it was too difficult for even us to face these kids and the loss of our son among them, but they looked genuinely glad to see us, and we couldn't possibly turn back now. As I stood there, those kids looked so little to me. They looked so innocent in that fifth grade classroom. I was reminded of a recent school paper in which Steven had to list something he had to work on before the transition to sixth grade. It was called his "Missing Piece." *"My missing piece isn't a big thing. It is a small part of me. I am a little forgetful. I have a hard time remembering a big list of things at once. Sometimes I have to ask someone to remind me. I do not mean to be forgetful. I am working on this."*

I thought the most important thing we could start out by saying was that "this was going to be okay." That we were okay and we were all going to get through this *together* and that it made *us* feel better just being with Steven's friends and that seeing the kids was a comfort to *us*. As we looked around the room, we saw that some of the students had already made their own memorial signs and messages at home over the weekend, and messages of love to Steven were everywhere. I had brought in a tri-fold poster board and asked the children who of the group could help me with a job. They raised their hands as school children do when volunteering, and I could tell that we already had their interest. I told them that there would be a huge celebration of Steven's life on Tuesday evening, and I was looking for decorations for the room, and that I needed friends who really knew him to make the special decorations. I said that I needed adjectives describing Steven to be decorated on the boards. I needed pictures and symbols of Steven's life that only they could help me with. When the boards were completed, I would need some friends to bring them to this celebration to display for all the other guests. Of course, I was referring to Steven's wake on Tuesday, and knew that calling it a "celebration" lessened the ominous tone to the service. Giving these kids a job would make them feel like they had helped, and were important themselves in this situation. I invited whoever wanted to come to Steven's "life celebration" to do so with their parents, and assured them that when they saw Steven, that he would look like his same old self, just sleeping. I told them that he would be wearing his travel baseball uniform if they chose to come up close to Steven lying there. Most importantly, I assured them that he would forever be their buddy and that he was watching over them even at that moment. And at that moment, I felt as though he *was* there with my husband and me, choosing my words for me somehow, guiding my actions, and it felt so right. One by one, the faces, looking so drawn and exhausted, looked a little less so. Our mission felt accomplished. Our goal, to help these children feel more secure and find a part and purpose in this horrific situation, was achieved. Later, I listened to voice mail messages from Steven's homeroom teacher, Mr. Ken Smith, and from a few of the parents of those students with whom we spoke who confirmed that, indeed, the children did benefit from our visit, that soon after we walked out the door, they got busy with their teachers making the posters, thinking of the adjectives, choosing the pictures that would be sent with the finished boards to the funeral home on Tuesday, that the entire mood of the classrooms had lifted a little. And knowing that we had made things just slightly better for these kids that day helped us enormously in our own pain.

* * *

CHAPTER 5: "I'M SORRY FOR MY LOSS"

"I'm so sorry about your son." "I'm so sorry for your loss." Over and over, we heard the painful sentiments of those who came to pay their last respects to our family of five. Our son was dead, and our family, as we knew it, was, too. And they were the ones who were sorry? No one could be more sorry than us.

Steven's wake lasted eight of the longest hours of our lives. Over 3,000 people came to say good-bye to our beloved son, and waited in lines for up to two hours. I felt guilty and sick to look down at what was left of our little boy. Dressed in his travel baseball uniform, Steven looked paper thin, every bone in his body having been basically flattened by the impact of the train. Brianna brought her favorite old baby blanket the next day to the funeral to cover up an especially awful break exposed in his arm, coincidentally the very same bone of the very same arm she had broken only the summer before. She said she understood how much that must have hurt him, and "wanted to make it feel better."

As I stood there receiving condolences, I was the one who wanted to apologize. *I'm sorry you had to wait in that god-awful line. I'm sorry you have to see my son like this. I'm sorry I let him walk out the door. I'm sorry to God for whatever I've done to deserve this. Did you hear me God? I'm sorry!!! Please don't punish us like this.* I couldn't bear to hear another "I'm sorry" from those who came to say good-bye to Steven. I needed to take the blame for this disaster. My face was gentle, my words few, but inside my head was spinning, my mind exploding as I'd accept condolence after condolence, greeting each solemn face, looking down at my Steven lying in a box. *What kind of a mother lets her son get hit by a train? Thank you for coming. Yes, I'm the mother whose son died. I didn't mean to let him die. He was killed, you see. Slammed by a train into a brick wall, in case you hadn't heard the horror story. I'm so sorry. Thank you for coming to my son's wake. Did I tell you he was killed? I'd never let my child die. A train killed him. I'm so sorry I couldn't save him. Thank you for coming. Next.*

The entire experience of our son's wake was so beyond surreal. Yet there we were, my husband and I stationed at the casket, there for the full impact of the worst night of our lives, a gulp of a water bottle every hour or so, our clothing, hands and faces covered with the tears of those who came to help us through. Our daughters took places outside of the immediate area of the casket, Frankie too upset and too aware of the enormity of the situation to come up close. I prayed that our families would keep watch over our sensitive 14 year-old in her fragile state, during what was surely the most torturous night of her life. Keeping my place by the casket, I couldn't be the comforting mother that Frankie surely needed that evening, the mom who should have been able to somehow make it better. It took all of Francesca's courage and strength to face the loss of her little brother, this boy who brought a little mischief and daring to his sweet, cautious, feminine older sister. Francesca "came out of her shell" when Steven came along, his flair for pranks like "mooning" his family and other boy shenanigans bringing an equal amount of head-shakes and suppressed giggles from her more reserved demeanor. Brianna, thankfully too little to absorb every horrific detail of this night, would come up to the casket and then wander around again, periodically watching or touching her dear "Stevie," her partner-in-crime, her fellow practical joker, her idol for simply being her big brother, lying there in the fancy wooden box with brushed nickel hinges, soon to be closed up and locked away, never again to share a pack of Fun Fruits or their dislike of any breakfast foods that couldn't accommodate chocolate chips. Her hero was gone forever.

Steven's closest friends congregated around the casket for periods of time, looking intently at their buddy lying there so still, the friend once full of energy who had just played baseball and video games with them days ago. The boys stood reading the flowers in the casket, one arrangement in particular that said "Best Brother," and studied the stuffed monkey Steven had affectionately once named, "Chim Chim," nestled in the arm of their little fallen comrade. They would take turns touching the cloth of his baseball uniform, touching him, seemingly okay with what would frighten many an adult; they stayed loyal and close all through the evening. At one point, Steven's friends leaned so heavily on the side of the casket that I thought the whole thing might topple over. Always curious, little boys, I thought as I shook my head and gently coaxed them away from leaning on the casket.

One by one, the families, friends, teachers, and acquaintances of our community slowly marched forward, offering a hug, sharing our tears, offering prayers and icons and small tokens of comfort and faith. We were surprised at how many brought their little ones along, maybe to bring them closure, definitely to bring us support and love. Even the paramedics and firemen who tried to help our son came by to offer a hug, their pained, stoic expressions as stiffly pressed as the uniforms they wore that night. *Thank you for trying. Thank you for trying to help save Steven. We know you did everything you could.* I don't know where the line began or ended; just that it seemed to go on forever.

When we finally went home that night, my husband and I talked for what felt like the first time since Saturday. "That wasn't even Steven in that box. That was only what was left of him." "I don't even associate the image of him tonight with our Steven. That wasn't our boy in there. We can't remember him like this." We were exhausted and disgusted and still in disbelief that we could be going through this nightmare, and that night, instead of sleeping, each of us wrote something for Steven's eulogy the next morning. The girls had written their good-byes, with extra copies to be encased in his casket forever, sealed away so that he would always have his sisters' sentiments next to his heart. Steve and I wanted our eulogies to focus on his life. We didn't want anyone, including ourselves, to simply remember him like that night.

The weather was bright and brisk the next morning, no day to be burying our child. It should've been pouring black rain. We arrived back at the funeral home, and it dawned on me that I would be soon counting down the minutes until I never saw Steven's angelic face again. All of a sudden, I had forty-five minutes to memorize the lines of his dimples, the small scars left from the chicken pox he had in kindergarten, dotting the side of his left cheek, the 22 tiny beauty marks sprinkled in various places on his face which he would affectionately call his "poo spots," laughing hysterically with his dad at the label. His cowlick was a circular little work of art adorning the front of his ever-shorn buzz cut, no question of which side he parted his hair, the cowlick made sure of that. He had just gotten his haircut the day before he was killed, readying himself for Easter, and had gotten in a little trouble from me when he came home from Gail, our hairdresser, and parked himself on our brand new couch to clip his toenails, leaving an assortment of nail remnants nicely tucked in the couch cushions, a surprise I would find weeks later.

There were several hundred friends and family members who came to the funeral home, and there would be a few thousand who attended the funeral Mass. I knew I couldn't waste my last precious moments with Steven by greeting all of these people again. They would have to understand that this was my time with my son. And so, instead of talking with anyone, I chose to sing a favorite bedtime song to him, just an old song which I had changed the words to for all three kids when they were first born, a sure soother whenever I couldn't get them to settle down. The song was, "You Are My Sunshine," and on this cruelest of sunny days, I sang it to Steven in the casket over and over, circling his cowlick with my index finger, studying the face I would never see again in this life. It was the last of my motherly efforts, to sing to him and comfort every pain he must certainly have felt being slammed and thrown by a 10,000 ton freight train.

You are my Steven, my dear, sweet Steven. You make me happy when skies are gray. You'll never know, dear, how much Mommy loves you. No one takes my sweet Steven away. The words to the last verse of my simple little song would soon take on new meaning, and would change my view on being told that I needed to say "good-bye" to my child. *You're darn right,* I would come to think. *No one takes my sweet Steven away. Nobody. My child is forever mine.* Did I realize it that day as they closed the lid of that fancy wooden box with brushed nickel hinges on my beautiful 11 year-old son? Of course, not. We were all in shock, moving in a trance that day and many, many days thereafter.

* * *

CHAPTER 6: COCOONS, COMFORTS AND OTHER "C'S"

It's strange, but I somehow remember those first days after Steven left us because of the clothing I wore. I remember grabbing comfort clothes, sad clothes, but I didn't wear black. The clothes I wore to the wake and funeral, and even some of the clothing I wore those first weeks, have either been stored away, thrown out, or donated because I can't even bear the memories of the days when I wore them. I remember the khaki pants and brown and green swirled shirt I wore to the funeral home on Easter morning. I remember throwing away the blood stained hooded sweatshirt I wore in the emergency room. Even though it was cleaned, that sweatshirt reminded me of hugging and kissing my dead child in my arms for the last time, and the thought of that jacket still makes me want to die myself.

No matter what we wore or how sick we felt, we derived great comfort in that we were never left alone those first days. A loving cocoon formed around us, and kept our house busy and bustling with noise and comfort. Soothing hugs and listening hearts remained close by. Our friends and family made sure we were never alone.

It was indeed therapeutic to have those we loved in our home. For the first days after the funeral, we'd gather to eat and talk of Steven, and just being together filled that time when we couldn't go back to any type of "normal" endeavors. We couldn't open the mail or go out of the house because that was "too real." It felt better to be nestled in this microcosm of non-reality where constant talk of Steven allowed us to pretend that he was just in the other room, at school, or had just done something funny last week and was somehow close by, not gone forever.

We donated Steven's funeral flowers to the local nursing home, partly because it seemed such a waste to let them die their own wilting death, and partly because we couldn't stand the smell in our house, which reminded us of the wake and funeral. We even planted what we thought might make it in our own garden. To this day, there are certain flowers, namely lilies and orchids, whose smell greatly bothers everyone in our family. If we receive a flower arrangement that includes those flowers, we immediately pick them out and get what we traumatically remember as the "smell of death" out of our home.

Our niece, Danielle DiBenedetto, thoughtfully made us all copies of the funeral songs such as "I'll Be There" by the Jackson Five, part of a CD of oldies that Steven listened to each night as he fell asleep. As an older cousin, Danielle's concern for the girls was gentle and caring. She was Francesca's Confirmation sponsor that week, and truly a warm comfort for both the girls.

We also greatly appreciated the food and dinners that would arrive daily at our door from friends and acquaintances. The meals came in such abundance that a network of our close friends from the community and school district organized the effort into a dinner rotation for us. They'd thoughtfully ask what our favorite foods were, or if we had a "taste" for anything special. All I wanted were Steven's favorite foods in our house, along with Steven there to enjoy them. I had a taste for nothing except life before April 19, 2003.

The constant flux of visitors to our home numbed those first days without our son and filled many otherwise empty hours alone. The big family dinners at our house with the hustle and chaos of many nieces and nephews also filled our home with needed "boy noise." Steven was suddenly missing in the white noise mix of our home, and our nephews helped fill it. They were present, supportive, a ready hug when we needed one, and made us realize how lucky we were to have so many wonderful nephews between our two large families.

Loved ones surrounded us during the day, but our nights proved to be especially fragile and full of panicky feelings. Our fear of the nighttime hours was compounded by repeated nightly thunderstorms those first weeks. Spring in Chicago usually manifests itself in unpredictable weather, but there were so, so many storms that spring, always seeming to begin around bedtime, that it seemed the gods were against us feeling any sort of calm once night fell and the eerie quiet took over. Unexpected changes in the weather and accompanying events at those times would soon become symbolic to me, although I didn't understand any of this early on. At that time, the nightly storms simply echoed our panic at concluding another day without our boy. And along with finding it impossible to find peace in going to bed, unsettling dreams and nightmares became a nightly ritual.

Steven appeared at the side of my bed that first Friday night. I couldn't speak at the joy I felt in seeing him again. He told me that God said he could come to visit on weekends if I could be brave during the week. I was thrilled to get any time possible with Steven, no matter when it was. He climbed onto my pillow, and I was holding him, much like when he was a toddler, his head on my shoulder, holding his chubby little hand.

Then, out of nowhere, headlights began shining through my bedroom window. I was worried as to who could be on our driveway, and told Steven I would be right back, as soon as I checked out the danger.

I ran downstairs, and opened the front door to find a woman in a car with her headlights on in our driveway, her blank face staring menacingly at me. I called out to her several times to identify herself or just to leave, but she only sat there staring. I began to scream at her to pull away, to leave my family alone, that we already had enough trouble and didn't need any from her. She only stared back for what seemed like an eternity, her headlights blinding my vision. I felt I had to stay there until the "danger" of her was gone, even though I desperately needed to get back to my precious few moments with my son. When she finally pulled away, I ran back upstairs to tell Steven that all was okay. I wanted to hold his hand again, but he had already disappeared.

When I woke up, my hand was curved into a "c", as if I really was holding Steven's hand. I was extremely upset that I had wasted all that time checking out the headlights and supposed danger when I could have been with him.

I lay in bed, crying and crying, begging God and whoever else would listen to let Steven come back, for even a few seconds. I felt that this wasn't a dream I had just experienced, but a visitation. I needed Steven to visit again, as in right at that moment. I needed to say so many things to him. I needed to apologize for wasting our time together with unfounded worry over a car in the driveway. I wondered how much precious time I wasted over the years by worrying about things that didn't matter, dangers that never were, but didn't realize the danger of a train that lived and breathed in my own backyard. I needed to give him a kiss on his soft cheek, to tell him that I loved him so much I couldn't live like this without him. I wanted one more chance to say that I was sorry I let him walk out the door, that I should've given him his first pop after Lent at home. I had so many questions, so many unanswered questions that were literally killing me inside. *Please, God, just two more minutes. Please Steven, come back. I'm so sorry I left you!*

The family and friends continued to come by during the day for a visit or to run an errand for us, and night after night featured dinners at our home. And although I had thus far felt comforted by all the daytime visitors who helped pass the hours while the girls were at school, one night the second week, I began to feel smothered by all the company. I found it draining to keep the conversations going, and began to feel like I was suffocating. It was hard to let go and cry or scream with dozens of people around me, and I wasn't the type to go hiding in my bedroom. The company had first kept us afloat, giving us strength, keeping the "Steven" talk alive, and that alone kept us going. And all that company masked the lack of conversation between my husband and me, the off-hours filled with little to talk about or comfort each other with. But the noise in the house, which had been such a source of life and support, suddenly exhausted me. Maybe true exhaustion was taking over. One night in particular, I couldn't wait for everyone to leave. My physical body was finally giving out to the constancy of my "on" button. I felt completely drained, and I couldn't wait for that constant "buzz" to become the silence of the emptiness inside of me. I couldn't wait to hear nothing. So after a family dinner one Sunday, we calmly and appreciatively asked everyone to give us some space.

I had no job at that time. I didn't have the slightest notion of what I would do with myself with each endless day waiting for the girls to get home from school, but I simply needed to be alone. It upset me beyond words to go into Steven's room because I would just lie there, smell his clothes and his bedding, which I refused to wash, and cry. I'd wander aimlessly around the house. We had accumulated hundreds of sympathy cards and letters, pictures drawn from little ones, mementos from the funeral, thoughts made for the girls from their friends and peers, inspirational verses, poems, grief books and other sentiments, and they all sat stacked on our dining room table. The sight of the piles made me realize how many days had passed since they all arrived, and how dormant they looked sitting there.

A few days later, while running a necessary errand to our local Walgreen's for one of the girls, I decided to stop at the Hallmark shop next door. I purchased several photo albums and scrapbooks. I brought them home, took a good long look at the stacks of cards, letters, pictures and prayer cards piled high, and just stared. For the first time since Steven was killed, I couldn't move. I froze in silence, absorbing the enormity of what had truly happened, the awareness that my life, as I knew it, was over. I walked over to the dining room table, put my head down on one of the piles and, finally alone, truly began to grieve in the silence of my home. My husband was out at the time, and I sat there with my head down for what seemed like hours, and cried and cried. I knew that putting together scrapbooks and albums wouldn't happen for a very long time.

For the next days, I cried non-stop. I cried from the moment the girls left for school till just before they came home, trying to put myself back together at that last hour before school let out so that they wouldn't come home to see how badly their mother was falling apart. I cried in my sleep, and for the hours I lay awake trying to sleep. I couldn't stop the tears, and knew I needed the release of shedding the anger I felt towards God and everyone and mostly myself for letting Steven out of my sight. *Because you truly aren't coming back, are you, sweetie?* In my exhausted state of mind, I would fool myself those first days into thinking that he was really just at school, and would get off the afternoon school bus with Francesca at 4:00. But he never did. During school hours when Steven normally wasn't home, I was able to mask the reality that he was never, ever coming home again.

For the most part, my husband sat numbly on the couch each day, staring into a void that I could not reach into and connect with. His little buddy was gone, and with it, an important gender connection. My husband thrived on the fact that his namesake loved sports as much as he did, and there was never any shortage of finding someone to watch a game with and talk baseball stats. Steve was a man who was meant to have a son. No mistake that he loved our daughters dearly and treasured their interests, but our son provided a vital link to what completed his dad; both were "all boy."

Although it had only been a short time, our family was encouraging Steve to go back to work, if only part-time, to give him a little distraction. We were barely speaking at home, both consumed by our own silent worlds of grief, neither strong enough to help the other, not registering that we needed each other so much but unable to cross over into the other's world of pain. There was also the silent "blame game" going on. I know that my husband wished I had told Steven he couldn't go to McDonald's that day. I know that I wished my husband had taken Steven to the college baseball game they were considering attending that day. Blame is a vicious card to play, and like guilt, generates useless emotions. But nonetheless, blame rears its head when there is no plausible reason to attribute to devastating loss. Blame robs you of objectivity and assigns fault where there is none. But for us, blame gave some explanation for why Steven was dead. We each blamed ourselves as we replayed the events of April 19th over and over. We couldn't accept the fate of that day, and we repeatedly relived each nuance of it, nothing ever making sense or offering us an ounce of comfort or logic. Anything, anything at all could have and would have changed that fateful day. The fingers were pointed everywhere, and none gave us the reasons we so needed to hear. When you lose your child, there is no reason good enough for their death.

With Steve headed back to work in a week or so, it was time for me to try to regain some control. I couldn't keep crying all day; I was completely exhausted. I needed to get back to some semblance of routine. I needed to get out the door. Although we knew it was important to place the kids back into their schedules as soon as possible, the thought of Steve and I resuming our usual routine was daunting. There would be no possibility of normalcy from here on end. After the loss of a child, the "normal" you once knew has no definition. But one thing certain about life is that it goes on whether you want it to or not. And so I decided to attend to some of the everyday tasks in life, which couldn't fall forever on the hands of our loved ones who were so helpful until this point. Having our extended family give us some space only allowed more time for us to fall apart in private. I wasn't sure what the balance was between having a support network around you versus having time to grieve alone. I also wasn't sure I was ready to head back out into our community per se; Lake Forest was a close-knit town, to say the least, and I felt like all eyes would be on me if I were out and about. Friends were inviting us as a family over for dinner to get us out. Banking needed to be done. Groceries weren't going to appear on our doorstep forever. So, I took a few baby steps. One didn't automatically lead to another. I crawled, I pulled myself up and then fell again. Indeed, "normal" would never again find its way into my vocabulary.

* * *

CHAPTER 7: MY BUDDY'S LIST

The days moved grudgingly forward, even though most times we didn't want the sun to rise the next morning. Indeed, there was no normalcy, no usualness about anything. We had simply "lived life" until the day someone took an eraser to our lives and removed a third of it. All we had was the rest of Steven's life around us, and no Steven here to live it.

We had no idea that the Krispy Kreme donuts he ate for breakfast or the chicken nuggets he had for lunch that day would be his last. We did not know that he wouldn't live to see his second day of travel baseball tryouts on Sunday, April 27th. We didn't know that his travel team would be wearing a black patch that simply said, "SBM 13" in memory of their teammate that summer. We didn't know we'd be returning his Easter outfit to the store unworn. Steven was on the cusp of so much when he died. Tender young life, but "life, interrupted," no less. There were no warnings to tell us that Steven Brian Malin, Jr. would die that day, leaving our world, our family, our home, forever. With a child's death from illness, there is the slow, agonizing realization that your child is slipping away as you stand helplessly watching. There is the fear of when "it" will happen. There are the countless visits to medical experts, to find the answers, to do anything to create the miracle, to beat the odds no matter what the cost. There are also the good-byes, the gut-wrenching words from the doctor that the battle is being lost, the gradual, slow, hopeless, senseless end to hope, the end to sense itself. No less painful. No more fair.

For us, we were moving, surviving, in complete and total shock. Our child was in the garage cleaning up his baseball equipment one minute and dead on a gurney an hour later. We got a phone call and fell off a cliff, and it's a fall you don't want to survive. There were no good-byes, no clues as to the fate that lie waiting for us.

I would move about the house finding all the parts of Steven's life still right where he left them. I would put the rest of his laundry away in his closets and drawers for no reason. I'd stand staring at his green and black hooded spring jacket as it hung on its familiar hook in our back hall closet. Spring was here, but Steven wasn't. I had hosted a garage sale exactly one week to the day before Steven was killed. Although I had planned to give his nicer hand-me-downs to our younger nephews, I had some play clothes and a few toys in the mix of the garage sale items. Not one thing of Steven's sold that day. Not one. *Hey God, did you know Steven was coming up to you that next Saturday? Did you make sure his things stayed in our loving hands? Is that how this works?* Indeed, I'd stare at all of his things, wondering why they were here and Steven wasn't.

I would check my email, glance at our list of screen names and see his emails accumulating into the several hundreds. I felt like I'd be betraying Steven's privacy by logging onto his screen name, but couldn't resist the chance to tap into another part of the life he so suddenly and violently left behind.

So one day those first few weeks, I did exactly that. I logged onto Steven's AOL account. I didn't know what I'd find on Steven's screen name. I carefully typed in his password, waiting, waiting. "Welcome, you've got mail." With those four words, I reopened Steven's world. A miniscule part of me felt guilty for invading his privacy. 99% of me was in pure pleasure to feel so close to my son for a little while. I actually spent hours on his screen name. I found his last email chains from the day before he died. I smiled as I read about a little girl in his class that he surely had a crush on. I laughed at the list of "blond jokes" and "Joe mama" messages he sent back and forth with his buddies. I cried hysterically reading the last emails he sent that fateful Saturday; not because they were anything of importance, but because they were the last words he typed just hours before he died. Then I found them. The email chains from Steven's friends regarding his death. A double click and I opened their world as well.

Among many, many touching email messages from kids who undoubtedly realized that one way or another their sentiments would eventually be read by our family, there were the immediate circulations of email chains sent around by the kids as early as the afternoon of Steven's death. In their own fifth grade way, they philosophically helped each other through their shock and grief, some sharing their religious faith in trying to understand how this could have happened, others just sharing thoughts on Steven himself. I got the feeling that many of the chains were sent without thought that Steven's family would be reading them; my son just part of the group buddy lists that went around. The kids, in their own grief, probably didn't even think about the fact that Steven's screen name was part of their circulating emails that afternoon and evening; that he tragically fell out of the loop and would never be part of their email chains again.

One by one, I read the messages, often astonished at the eloquence of the young writer, sometimes sensing that the words of wisdom on death and dying originated from a caring parent's words to their child that day. At times, I sat stunned that I was even reading reflections on death from these little people, and that the death was my son's.

"Steven was taken up to heaven to be with God today. He will always be an angel over our shoulders."

"God took Stevie Malin away from us because he loved him so much. We all know that he has gone to a better place to be with God. We will always remember Stevie and his bright smile and funny personality. Please pray for the Malin family in their time of grief and sorrow."

"Steven Malin was a really great kid and no one could ever forget him. We want to take a minute today and pray for all of those who are affected by his death. We pray for the Malin family for being so strong at a time like this and we will pray for all of

us friends who have lost him. But God does everything for a reason so maybe God has something better planned for Steven in heaven. Rest in peace, Stevie."

"Dear Steven, we all love you and are sad that your time has come to join God. We will see you when our time comes to leave this earth and go to heaven too. We will love you forever. From all your friends."

"Dear Mr. and Mrs. Malin, I am very sorry that your son has died. I have been crying all day since I heard about it. If Steven's baseball team was losing 6-0, he would always look for the positive, put his rally hat on and encourage his teammates. Steven was the best artist and baseball player I have ever known. I am so sorry."

"Dear Malin family, I am so sorry. I love you so much. Stevie was one of my best friends. He was a good boy. I know you miss him a lot and so do I. I liked him a lot."

"Dear Mr. and Mrs. Malin, I will miss Steven forever. He was really nice and could cheer anybody up when they were sad. I remember when we were little and Steven taught me how to tie my shoes. I wish he were still here."

"Dear Malins, I hope you are reading this. I am so sorry that the train killed Steven today. He was the best friend ever. He always had a way of cheering everyone up. He wasn't ever mean or selfish. I think Steven was an angel sent from God. I guess heaven was getting boring with only old people up there. They needed some fun and joy up in heaven so they chose Steven Malin. Maybe Steven was here such a short time because he was only here to teach us something. I think it was to live life to the fullest because it may be the last time you can."

"Steven...Special...Talented...Energetic...Violinist...Enthusiastic...Never gave up...I hope you like what I made about my best friend, Stevie Malin. How lucky everybody was to know him."

"God stole Steven from our lives. He deserved to live a longer life but I guess that God loved him more than we did. God bless you as you live in eternity with God."

"Dear Malin family, I wrote this for Steven. Steven means, "Super Star Athlete... The Best Smile...Excellent Baseball Player...Very Determined...Excellent Friend to Have...Number 1 Forever."

"Dear Mr. and Mrs. Malin, I wonder why Steven had to die. God must have something waiting for him that he wanted him to have right away, so God took his life. Steven will always be loved."

"Dear God, I wish you had let me say good-bye to my friend, Stevie. I will never see his million dollar smile again and I am so sad and tired from crying. I haven't smiled in a long time now."

As I read on and on, one of his Steven's classmates IM-ed in a "Hi, who is this?" and I sent back, "Hi, it's only Mrs. Malin." After a long pause, he IM-ed back, "Oh, I'm so sorry to have bothered you, Mrs. Malin." I didn't want him to be sorry or think that he bothered me. I was the adult out of place in the world of 5th grade email. Yet there I was, deriving so much comfort and releasing so much emotion that day I spent in the world of Steven's AOL. I printed out all the messages, the jokes, the email chains. Creating hard copies of everything preserved them forever for me. Through this little exercise, I found hours of respite in my personal storm. I actually felt "normal" taking a glimpse into my son's normal life. And it was through spending the day in Steven's "life" versus the endless days of his "death" that finally sparked a little life in me again. I wondered what else would bring me this new and welcomed feeling. I knew I wanted it again and again.

We never deleted Steven's online account. We still have his AOL screen name to this day. Once in a while, I will send some little poem or thought to Francesca and Brianna, and I'll send one to Steven as well. I go on his screen name once a week or so to clear out his never ending junk mail, but even the "junk" is a sign that parts of his life go on. This aspect of Steven 's world will never go away, never die because we don't let it. I can't imagine not having his screen name amongst the list on our family's AOL. When I sign on, I see his along with ours, and know that it is only right that his screen name remain. Over the first year after losing him, a few of his friends continued to email us on Steven's account. They eventually started emailing directly to my husband or me, or even one of the girls, but no matter whose screen name they use, we cherish the fact that they want to keep in touch.

That special day, so long ago now, Steven was just a click away from me, a normal little boy who loved Krispy Kreme donuts, chicken nuggets and playing on AOL. A simple click away versus the infinite distance from here to heaven, and I loved it.

* * *

CHAPTER 8: ASSAILED BY HAIL

I realized that the reprieve I felt during that time spent on Steven's AOL account was due to the feeling of him being "alive." Concentrating on Steven's life felt like a "lifeline" itself. The month of May brought constant reminders of Steven's death, and I wanted so badly to go back and hide on the AOL. We spent a good deal of that month attending memorials arranged in Steven's honor. We tried to leave our oppressive house a little bit, but the outings didn't go well. Living in a house with one member suddenly gone was stifling, thick with darkness. Leaving that house proved to be disastrous as well.

We decided to accept our first invitation to have a quiet family dinner at the home of our good friends, Peggy and Dan Schweller, with a few other families who were celebrating the 42nd birthday of our wonderful friend, Carl DiTomasso. Although we were far from being in any mood to celebrate, Carl had been with us since the first moments at the hospital. He waited with Steven's body in the emergency room till the coroner and then the funeral home arrived while we went home to our other children, and helped our immediate family see to so many details of Steven's services. Carl showed friendship beyond what friendship should ever ask of you, and we thought that spending his birthday with him was not only what we needed to do, it was where we wanted to be. It was a warm spring evening, Peggy and Dan lived close by, and we thought a change of scenery would be good for us all.

While the kids played, the adults relaxed with a cocktail, and it actually felt good to listen to different conversation. One of the nicest parts about being with these friends was that our children's ages all fell within a few years of each other, and getting together was easy and natural. Except that this night, the first with us together again, there was one boy missing — ours.

I found myself looking at the cluster of little ones as if someone had cut out a big hole in the picture.

We stopped our conversation to make a birthday toast to Carl, and the next words I heard would turn the rest of the night into a blur. In the midst of the toast, Carl joined in and said that they had some surprising news, but good news, news that they had waited to share until they thought we were ready to hear it. Robin, Carl's wife, was unexpectedly pregnant with twins, and their family would soon grow to five children. Our three children and their three children had always gotten along more like cousins than friends; we vacationed with them and loved spending time together. That night, I couldn't grasp onto still another shake-up in the once familiar world I knew. We were families, each with three children, who were steadfast friends for seven years. Our family structures fit together perfectly. That night, although I felt genuinely happy for them, I felt sorrier than ever for myself. Cheated of losing my child, my only son, and going home with only two children that evening, wondering why God would give Carl and Robin two more. Where was the justice? Why was I being punished like this? That night, instead of sleep, I counted any and all mistakes I must have made in my life to deserve this most cruel penance from God — taking Steven away.

As we drove the short ride home, our girls spoke continuously about the twins coming. They were excited about the thought of new babies on the way. Evidently, they had also been thinking of us having another baby, even adopting a baby, to help fill our void, and voiced their desire during this car ride. Although I would have done anything to bring our daughters happiness once again, my husband and I knew that trying to have another child would not be any quick fix, and would definitely never replace Steven. Although we knew that "replacing Steven" wasn't our girls' goal, bringing a baby into this world, under any circumstances, would also bring stress and responsibility that we were in no emotional shape to handle. This would be unfair to everyone, especially an innocent child.

Steve went back to work part-time that next week, and I continued on same path of tears as the week before, knowing that my first attempt at a real family outing was a complete failure. Going back out in public thus far proved to be a bad idea. Maybe we would never be comfortable in social settings, and others would always feel uncomfortable around us. For the time being, I decided to try to simply tackle the basic needs of our household and help our family to begin to function again.

The first time I returned to the grocery store, a family-owned chain we frequented called "Sunset Foods" in Lake Forest, I cried the whole way through my attempt at shopping. Panic had set in again. Who would I buy chicken nuggets for? As in any household, I bought certain favorite foods for each member of our family, and one of my son's favorites was chicken nuggets. Would I never buy Steven's favorite foods again? Death not only takes away the very person we love, it takes away all of the small but wonderful pleasures that come with having that person in your life. With a child, it's buying special treats, making their favorite dinner, packing a lunch you know they love and can't wait to tear into at school.

I stumbled through the frozen aisle. Why didn't I buy the Dove ice cream bars the kids wanted the last time we all went grocery shopping together? Although Bri had begged for them, Steven responsibly put them back in the case, explaining in his 11 year-old mature voice, "Mom's right, they're too expensive." I would give my arms and legs to be having that conversation again right now. And I would say "yes" this time. Life is too short to say no to ice cream, or much else, I knew now so painfully well. It could all be taken away in a heartbeat, this fall off a cliff that you somehow survive but wished you hadn't. I could barely make my way down each aisle. I stood with my head down, paralyzed and crying. The manager of the grocery store, Steve Davis, who was also a family friend, gently came up and took the cart from my hands and wheeled it the rest of the way to the checkout counter. Looking back, I don't think I could have found my way out of the store without his assistance. As I wrote out my check, the clerk innocently asked me how I was, as I'm sure she asked every customer that day. I wanted to say, "How do you think I am now that my son is dead?" Instead, I said nothing and wrote out my check, careful not to look up and let her see my face, more tears silently streaming down. Angrily, I stormed out of the store. Angry at no one in particular, except everyone and everything in the world. I got in my car, screamed in a pain that nothing would seem to lessen, and drove home. Indeed, death hung over me everywhere I went at that time.

Mother's Day was a few days away, and I couldn't bear the thought of it. Not only would it be the first holiday without Steven, it was the last holiday I ever felt like celebrating again. Mother's Day was, to me, a time of reflection, looking back at the lives of my children that year, how they had grown and changed, accomplished and learned.

My dad insisted on taking everyone out for an extended family dinner, and it was the last place I wanted to be. The night before, I lay in bed and found it hard to breathe, literally. I tossed and turned and felt sick thinking of Mother's Day without Steven. There would be no "reflection" on Steven this year. He would never "grow" again or "learn" again. Three weeks before Mother's Day would be the last day I saw my little boy change and take one step closer to the rest of his life. As sleep again eluded me, I tortured myself, as I had gotten so good at doing. *What kind of a mother was I, anyway? Was I a mother who let her child out of her sight only to be killed by a train? God help me, why did I say "yes" for him to walk to McDonald's? I could have said "no." I was so overprotective that I said "no" all the time.* Here I was, thinking I was a mother who tried to do everything right, keeping her children safe, priding herself that they hardly ever got sick or hurt. With Mother's Day just hours away, I felt like the biggest failure of a mother in the universe. I didn't deserve to celebrate Mother's Day. *I only deserved to die. I failed to keep my child safe.*

As those minutes went on, I felt a tight constriction in my chest that I could only attribute to a heart attack. I had no pain in my shoulder, only an increasing tightening in my mid chest area that I was sure was the onset of a heart attack. And the sad thing is, I didn't care. I watched my husband sleeping next to me, and thought that in the morning he would simply find me dead next to him and go through Mother's Day without me. I knew that I didn't deserve to be honored with the other mothers, so somehow this would be better. I closed my eyes and awaited my fate, doing nothing to alert my family to my symptoms. Little did I know that the pain I felt was actually the start of an ulcer, which would bleed and come to full-blown proportion over the next few months. My heart wasn't tearing apart in the true sense, only figuratively. My stomach would soon bleed. My heart had been "bleeding" for weeks.

We went to Sunday Mass as a family for Mother's Day, against my wishes. I felt sick again, going through a day of motions without emotions. I sat in church and stared at the aisle in which Steven's casket stood just a few short weeks ago. I couldn't listen to our priest tell of the riches of motherhood and how rewarding a role in life it was. I felt the poorest of poor, the weakest of failures, and wanted to take the pulpit again, only to tell the whole congregation how I had failed, how this seeming pillar of strength a few weeks ago had already crumbled. I wanted to tell them how sorry I was that I was here today with all the other mothers who deserved Mother's Day, not this pathetic imitation of a mother who couldn't keep her child safe.

In looking back, I realize that my feelings were coming on so strongly and swiftly that I felt like a different person from one minute to the next. One was overcome with guilt, one basically still in shock, another completely out of touch with reality. I was grasping onto moments of a "living" Steven, wondering how I could get more of that and less of death at every turn. I couldn't sort out my emotions, one from the other, couldn't forgive myself for any of them. I was half in hysterics, half dead, and didn't know where to turn first. Nothing had any semblance to the old Maria. I went from being a proud mother of three who was high on life to some unrecognizable face in the mirror. Pain was everywhere. I didn't want to be a mother of two. I wanted life before April 19, 2003.

I didn't want Mother's Day without my own child, or the Fourth of July without the fireworks of my little boy who lived life with such gusto. Mother's Day ended with the now familiar exhaustion and little coherence of another day in my personal horror story. Once again, I lay in bed awake for hours, the dreams visiting me.

I was at the playground at Everett Elementary School (the local grade school that all three children attended). Brianna wanted to play on the swing set and asked me to watch her go down the slide. I was cheering her on as she climbed the steps, then went into shock as I saw her come into view. She sat at the top of the slide, holding her arms around the lifeless body of Steven. She looked so happy to have him there with her, and said they were ready to go down. I began crying and screaming for her to stop, and let her brother go. She insisted on going down and down the slide again, each time with her beloved Steven in her arms. She was constantly at the top of the slide and I couldn't stop her. She smiled and told me that it was all right, that she wanted Steven to play with her no matter if he were alive or dead. I tried reasoning with Brianna, explaining that Steven couldn't play anymore. Finally, she ended her trips down the slide and came to face me alone. She finally showed her face, tears flooding her small cheeks, and she collapsed into my arms. I told her how sorry I was that I let Steven die, and that I would make sure she had lots of friends to play with, but that she just couldn't play with Steven anymore. Slowly, she turned with me to look at the slide and Steven's body had already disappeared. We walked arm and arm back to our car.

I awoke in a cold sweat, the weekend having drained me of my last shred of energy. I would awaken most nights over the next weeks with the cold sweats, the toll of the nightmares and sleeplessness accumulating into constant feelings of exhaustion and anxiety. I wondered how the mind played out the fears of the day through the dreams at night, how my physical body would be able to withstand the long-term effects of the mental strain on my psyche, how I would ever come to find rest or peace again.

On an especially dark, gloomy afternoon in May, my husband and I prepared to attend the Lake County, IL Coroner's hearing into the death of our little boy. The word "coroner" itself sounded completely impossible to use in the same sentence with our son's name. Whose life *was* this? It continued to feel like anyone's but ours. We dreaded the thought of having to go to the coroner's inquest, but knew that the information presented there would fill in some of the missing facts surrounding Steven's accident. Because of the circumstances of Steven's death, it was customary for the county coroner's office to conduct such a hearing. A jury panel would decide on the exact cause of death, and rule as to whether an additional investigation was recommended. Other than the documentation we received from the county, we had no idea what to expect at the inquest, no idea until a paralyzing phone call I would receive the day before.

With ominous weather looming overhead, I was in my car on the way to pick up Brianna from Everett Elementary, a route we usually walked together in good weather, when I got a call from the deputy coroner, a polite but young-sounding woman who asked if I had a few minutes to talk. I thought she would be preparing me as to the length of the hearing, when to arrive, how the deliberation would take place, and so on, but I was again stopped cold when I heard what she had to tell me.

"Mrs. Malin, I know this will be rather disturbing for you to hear with no prior warning, but I feel it necessary to tell you of some of the details which will come out during tomorrow's proceedings, details of the multiple injuries suffered by your son, as well as our office's documentation as to the cause of his death. Although no autopsy took place per your family's request, I was the one who conducted the necessary post-mortem lab testing on Steven, the results of which will be part of the details of tomorrow's hearing." I sat in the car in another state of complete shock, wondering how I would continue to drive to pick up my daughter from school, sit in the car rider's line waiting for her, maintain control of my car at all. I asked her to go on, hoping that I could go on, driving, listening, not believing what was happening — again. How could I, who could barely stand to watch one of my children fall down, skin a knee, need a stitch, somehow sit calmly in my car and listen to the graphic details of my little boy's injuries, the mutilation of his four-foot five inch tall, 75 pound body by this monstrous locomotive.

As the deputy coroner detailed the findings, the sky grew even darker, opening up as if the heavens once again could not bear to remain quiet since the death of Steven Brian Malin, Jr. By this time, my little girl sat patiently in the back seat of the car, surely wanting to tell me about her day at school, quietly waiting until I was off the phone with whomever I was listening to so intently at that moment. As I drove, a violent storm threatened, hanging in a black sky, and I shook with nausea at the details of my son's injuries, one after another, the reality of what happened to him hitting me like the cracks of thunder, one after another, overhead. I should have hung up the phone and called the deputy coroner back later when I was safely at home and away from Brianna, but I was worried that I wouldn't catch her back before the end of the day. She had left me a few voice mails, and until that call in my car, we hadn't been able to connect live. I didn't want to risk coming to the hearing the next day unprepared, although I had no idea what "prepared" even meant.

I hung up as we rounded the corner on our way toward home when sudden, violent hail began pummeling my car, my sweet Brianna screaming in fear in the back seat, me barely being able to maintain my own control or the control of our car. "We're almost home, we're almost home," I kept shouting, as the hail continued its assault on us. I could barely park in my garage, coming very close to scraping the side of my doors pulling in. *God help us! Please, please God, help us! We need you!* Why was this nightmare never ending? Why were we being punished over and over? I lay my head down on the steering wheel, sobbing and shaking and feeling again like I could not leave our home without the heavens falling down on me. I hugged Bri as we entered the house, my young, frightened girl, reassuring her that we were indeed safe from the hail now, believing nothing of what I was saying. All I knew was that Steven was dead, the skies had beaten down on us, and in the last fifteen minutes I now knew every sorted last detail of his suffering injuries, and would face even more graphic detail the next day.

The coroner's inquest would indeed prove to be another day of "hail," another round of horrific assault on what little strength was left of us; my brother, Gene, sitting on one side of me, my husband on the other, all of us expected to maintain some level of composure while listening to the details of Steven's demise, wondering how life had come down to this last shred of feigned civility. We sat perfectly still, and after a very long morning, the jury did come to the conclusion that the facts of Steven's death warranted further investigation into the railroad's actions that day. We came to our own conclusion; that life, again, was over, and nothing would bring Steven back to us. No "further investigation," no inquisitions, no apologies from anyone, public or private, would allow Steven to walk through the front door again, to run late for baseball practice again, to gripe about practicing his violin again.

For some reason, the hail continued to come that season, a symbolic and suspicious sign that life was unsettled, on the verge of breakdown at any moment, and we came to feel that the hail itself was a message from Steven, the cold, hard shards of reality that he, too, did not understand this surreal ending to his young life.

* * *

CHAPTER 9: LIFE VS. DEATH — THE CROSSROADS AT THE CROSSING

I spent my days sitting at the kitchen table, going through sympathy cards, reading them, re-reading them, wondering how I got to this place, finding little else to be of any value in doing. Some of the cards I received spoke to me more than others.

> *"I seldom ask for miracles, but today one would do, to have the front door open and see you walking through. A million times I've missed you, a million times I've cried. If love alone could save you, you never would have died. In life I loved you dearly, in death I love you still. In my heart you hold a place that no one else could ever fill. It broke my heart to lose you, but you didn't go alone. Part of me went with you the day God called you home."*
>
> *Author Unknown*

After Steven was killed, I had constant feelings of guilt and worry that no one was taking care of him, that he was somewhere all alone and needed one of his parents to be with him. Although I now see that these were the immediate, irrational, desperate feelings which accompany such extreme loss, they sent me agonizing guilt, day and night. I felt that because I was Steven's mother, I was forever responsible for taking care of him, even in death, and that he was somewhere far away, alone and needing me. After all, he was only eleven years old. Who was with him? Who took care of the little children of heaven? I spent my life taking care of my three children, and now I couldn't get to one of them because the Grim Reaper had come and snatched him away.

I also secretly felt like no one in my family could really understand the depth of my pain. When I was alone, I would scream my fury, the longing for my little boy that I was sure no one could imagine the extent of. I would hear stories of other parents who had lost a child, because those stories continued to come out of the woodwork, and I would just die over and over again. Silently, I thought that these other parents could never know what I was going through, that they couldn't possibly have loved their child as much as I loved Steven. At times, I would scream to my sister, Diane, or my brother, Gene, "You have no idea how much I loved that boy!" I was so completely drained of energy that I now realize I was drained of sense as well. All parents love their children. Looking back, I simply could not find adequate words to verbalize my own personal pain. I couldn't tell the world how much it hurt to have Steven gone. I couldn't imagine that anyone, including my own husband and children, felt the loss and obligation that I felt as Steven's mother.

I would look at my husband and our two daughters and begin to calculate in my overwrought, unstable mind that one of us should take care of the girls here and the other should go to Steven and take care of him. It was not right that he was alone and not with the four of us anymore. I constantly thought about going to him. Day and night, I needed to get to him. I thought that I couldn't live in this earthly world without him. The few moments of respite that I tried so hard to hang onto were overshadowed daily by his death. I honestly thought that any good and caring mother would think the same way that I did. During those first few months, my image to the outside world was that of this devoutly faithful Catholic Christian who knew that my son was safely in heaven with God. The "inside" hysterical me believed that I still needed to parent my child and wondered how I could continue to do just that. Down deep, I wanted to find a way to be with Steven if he could no longer be with me. My nightmares told me that Steven was cold, hard, dead, alone, and I was the one who could make him safe and warm again. For what I thought was a good and honorable reason, *I needed to die.* I needed to care for my son in death so that he was not alone. With every breath I took, I thought about going to him. C.S. Lewis writes, *"God whispers in our pleasures, but shouts in our pains."* I truly thought I was hearing God telling me to go to Steven. I felt a calling, a strange, unfamiliar calling to satisfy the yearning for a child that could not be let go; and, in essence, a yearning to die myself. And I thought that God was leading me to this. I had been trying so hard to hear God. He felt so removed from me. Yes, *I have needed You!*

The first time I truly thought I might die was the night before Mother's Day as I lay in bed for hours with those grimacing chest pains. I felt an odd calm knowing that I could soon be reunited with my son if I just stayed quiet and didn't tend to the cause of my pain. The next morning, I spent my Mother's Day feeling disappointed that the pain was not some tragic cardiac arrest that would join me with the child I so missed and needed, and thought needed me.

I soon started to incorporate this yearning to die with my daily activities, and thought about it constantly. Because my life was in true "crisis," and the word crisis comes from the Ancient Greek word meaning "to decide," I can look back now knowing that my life was hanging on a cusp. Unfortunately, the cusp at that time became deciding whether to live or die. I wondered if I could really, truly live on without Steven. *I didn't realize that I could keep him here with me.* If I could die in a car accident, I thought, I would reunite with Steven. I spent a lot of time wondering about this most real desire. I needed to go to my son if I couldn't have him here with me. The only thing that would occasionally snap me back to reality in at this time of confusion was being with my two daughters, knowing how much I would miss them if I left this earth now. I never entertained the notion that they might actually miss me if I died; that they also needed *me*. In so many ways, I had felt like I was a failing mother anyway, unable to truly help my daughters through their pain. In my exhausted and desperate state, I also figured that there were so many family members and friends who, in addition to their father, would take great care of the girls that they would never even miss me being there, and that they would somehow understand that I needed to finish taking care of their brother.

Indeed, I was not only in crisis, but out of touch with reality and reason, not even able to objectively make minor decisions, let alone this momentous one. I thought that if I joined Steven, I would be free to care for the one who was alone, the one who must surely be missing the care of a parent. These feelings of despair culminated into one defining event, one afternoon, some weeks after Steven's death.

We lived extremely close to the train station where Steven was killed. In fact, we had to cross those very tracks day in and day out to get anywhere in our town. We even had to cross the tracks at a few different intersections; it was unavoidable, and it proved to be unbearable each day to drive from our home.

One day, I had just dropped Bri off to play at a friend's house near, where else, the railroad tracks. My plan was to head to the grocery store after the drop-off and pick something up to fix for dinner. I approached the railroad tracks, albeit at another intersection, and saw the gates coming down. With no one ahead of me, I knew I would be sitting there by myself, first in line, nothing to block my view of the train, for at least a few minutes until the train passed. Although I would normally be in a panic, a strange calm took over me. I began to calculate. I devised my strategy to join my son who so needed me. I would go around the gates.

Indeed, I had enough seconds before the train reached my crossing that I could move my car up and be hit. I would die the same death as Steven. In moments, I would be with the son I missed so much. I would be able to continue being a mother to him, to care for him in death as I thought was my responsibility, to fill my undeniable longing. I inched my car close enough to see down the tracks to the headlight of the train approaching, and knew all I had to do was turn the wheel and hit the gas. I would join Steven. I felt my breathing easy and rhythmic. I felt peace knowing that I could have control once again of this uncontrollable situation. There is power in that feeling of control. We never feel that we will be in the power seat when we die. Death knocks at our door without ever being invited. Here, in my car, I knew the power that someone must feel over death when one considers suicide. *Death will not knock at my door again. I will choose. I will have the control over my destiny. Steven was taken from me, but I will have the power to change my own life's course with one hit of this gas pedal.*

Obviously, I changed my mind. Yes, I was a victim. I was a victim of the horrendous, unfathomable, unholy contemplation of committing suicide. The moment that I stopped myself, I literally gripped the steering wheel and floored the brake pedal. I thrust it down so hard and held it for what felt like an eternity, far beyond the train crossing my path. Cars had accumulated in back of me by the time I finally pulled slowly and safely ahead. And all I thought about were my two precious girls. What whipped past my mind in those moments were their faces. I pictured them as babies, as little girls, as the daughter who played happily at her friend Emily's house down the street that very moment, as the teenager who waited patiently at home for me to arrive with groceries for dinner. I sobbed in my car as I thought of these precious children who needed me to hold that brake pedal down and stop. *I stopped, God, I stopped. Did you see? Even without You there for me, I stopped.* My dear, dear daughters, the true innocent victims of this horrific tragedy, needed both their mom and dad to get them through. And I would be here for them.

The defining moment of the journey of my son's death to that day was when I decided that I should *live*. I would not go to Steven. I would not be a victim. I would also not make my family a victim of this irrational action. I would be a survivor. I would survive this insurmountable moment. *I would find a way to keep Steven with me. Here.* Here where my daughters needed me. Here where I needed to finish raising them. Here where I wouldn't bring them any more heartache by my death. Here because my husband couldn't accept the burden of my dying, either.

I would keep Steven here with me. There are few times in life of this magnitude where we come to a crossroads, in true crisis, a place where we find ourselves needing to change the way we have lived thus far, and how we will now live from this moment forward. This moment at the train tracks, refusing to pull my car up and be done with this earthly life and join what I thought would be eternity with Steven, was what defined my future path, the remainder of my journey here as wife, mother to Francesca and Brianna, and somehow be a "me" who would move through life again with goals, direction and strength. It is said that the most common result of severe crisis is not post-traumatic stress disorder (although my hair loss, nightmares and anxiety attacks would have made me think otherwise), it is "personal growth." The crossroads that severe trauma brings to our lives causes us to move in a new direction, to allow new aspects of our being to emerge if we let them.

And so, it took me to say "no" to this disastrous act to say "yes" to what defines me today — forever a mother of three, forever Steven's mother, knowing that no one will take that away from me. I can live on. I choose life. *No one takes my sweet Steven away.* To fill what looks like the biggest, blackest hole in your life takes courage and a new you. I sincerely feel that an important "old" me died that dark day that I contemplated taking my own life. That "me" thought that my relationship with my son hinged on the "old me" getting to the "old him." But we weren't the same anymore. I was no longer the mother to the human form of Steven, and he no longer needed me to mother him in that way because he now lived in eternity, no longer encumbered by our human existence. He didn't need a mom who made his lunches and got him to sports on time, but he still needed me. He needed me to go on in my new life here on this earth. I didn't realize until that day that I could "move forward" without Steven and not callously "go on" without him.

To say that I was deeply changed by that day at the train crossing is such an understatement. I also realized that day that I needed outside help. I needed to have a safe place to talk about the extreme emotions I was feeling. I didn't know what to do with the epiphany I had just experienced. I couldn't just drive home that afternoon, and magically, all would be well. I had a family waiting there who needed a wife and mother. I didn't exactly know who she was just yet. But I was willing to try, for all the right reasons. Taking my own life would only be wrong, and would make a terribly wrong situation only worse. I owed my family more than that. I felt shaky and deeply disturbed as I walked back through the door that evening, too strung out to even begin to describe what had just happened to me. Instead, I was silent, but silently embracing my family again, watching them at dinner, feeling like I would be here for good now. Knowing that "here" was where I needed to be.

* * *

CHAPTER 10: FINALLY, GRIEF

After the episode at the train crossing, I thought more seriously and more urgently about getting into grief counseling. I felt more focused having gotten past that tremendous incident, but knew that getting into some type of grief therapy would help me sort out what was happening at home, and to me personally, in my heart and in my head. Although I knew that "life" was calling me, I just couldn't label that new life yet. I now understood that Steven no longer needed me to mother him. My girls, however, did. They were sad, confused, and needing support that I hadn't been able to give them. They had a mother who was walking around as this half-person looking to define her other half, but didn't have the "how to" of it figured out yet. I couldn't provide help to my hurting children when I needed so much help myself.

I also had become physically sick. I contracted a mild case of the Haemophilis B or HIB, virus from someone, one of the 3,000 or so people who hugged me, kissed me, and sadly left me with a dull, throbbing sore throat that never seemed to go away. When I finally went to my doctor, she ran some tests to see if I had a latent strep throat, only to call me days later and tell me that someone had given this childhood illness to me. The kids didn't understand much of this aftermath. I truly didn't, either.

Frankie and Bri had been offered assistance by the social workers at their schools, and quite frankly, didn't seem to want grief counseling in that form, or to open up to what were strangers to them just a few short weeks ago. They seemed more focused on getting back into some semblance of a normal routine at home, at school, with their extra-curricular activities and their friends.

I remember Francesca asking me one day when I would wear make-up again. I guess I didn't realize that she even noticed that I wore make-up every day, or that I had now stopped wearing it. I made up an excuse of what I thought she wanted to hear in that my eyes were bothering me, and that the make-up only worsened the situation. What I should have honestly said is that I couldn't stop crying. Why bother applying mascara when it would be washed away within minutes every morning? Even when the children asked why I was crying, I would lamely say that I had a headache or a stomachache. Why couldn't I tell them that I missed their brother so much that every part of my body and spirit felt broken and the tears wouldn't stop coming?

The girls, themselves, hardly cried. They remained stoic for the most part, and it would only be revealed years later that they wanted to be strong for Steve and me, that they didn't want to cause us any more trouble by crying and adding to our burden. Looking back, I wish I had been more honest about my own tears, or encouraged my daughters to release theirs. I wish I had been more present for them and more authentic about my own emotions. All of our tears could have pooled together and helped cleanse our pain as a family. When one member of a family dies, the family, as it was, dies as well. We should have been trying to transition into a new family instead of trying to maintain the old. Reaching a state of authenticity, whether in emotion or communication, is so terribly difficult in times like this. I couldn't bring myself to tell them one iota of my near suicide experience at the tracks. I had just been through this extreme metamorphosis, yet couldn't even imagine sharing the incident with my family, not even my husband. So to Steve and the girls, I still outwardly maintained my old self, a half and broken self who needed professional help.

I realized that there wasn't really anyone in my immediate world who I felt could listen to me in the objective way a professional could. I felt like I needed help to make the Maria who was "born" at the railroad crossing materialize, so she could be a better parent, a more emotionally present mother to her daughters who deserved nothing less.

Friends and family all had resources that they suggested over and over, and up until then, I just wasn't ready for them. "Willow House," in a suburb of Chicago, was frequently mentioned as a place where I could bond with other families who had lost a child. I wasn't sure that I wanted to bond with those families yet. At that time, I didn't want to admit that I was now part of a new club, with members who sadly belonged because they had "lost." Maybe that was part of being in denial early on. Like the stages of dying, the stages of grief manifest themselves in unusual ways, often reappearing and jumping in and out of the picture and causing us to move back to denial and forward to acceptance at any unexpected juncture. This is how I initially felt about group grief counseling. Did I really want to admit that I belonged in a group of parents who had lost a child? I guess I didn't, and maybe didn't want counseling in any shape or form because, like my daughters, I wanted our old life back, plain and simple. I didn't want four with a hole in the middle. I wanted five. I also hated the term "bereaved mother." It sounded like I had died as well. Bereavement equaled death to me, and I had enough death to last a lifetime.

So, although group counseling didn't sound like a good fit, I gave in and sought out a private grief counselor. On a sunny Saturday that spring, I checked into a dark office in a nearby suburb and poured my story out to a perfect stranger. I went to see a female counselor, and specifically sought out one who was a mother because I thought she would understand me more easily.

With nowhere to begin with her but at the beginning, I laid out the story of Steven's accident. Just rehashing the details proved to be near fatal for me that day, and as the hour unfolded, for the grief counselor as well. She cried and cried and could barely speak through her own tears. I found myself handing her a Kleenex more often than I grabbed one for myself. I watched her mascara run, in a sad sort of way, because I knew she should be catching my tears, and I heard myself telling her that it was "okay, really okay," yet those were the words she should have been saying to me. I walked out, completely drained, and never went back there again.

Then I tried joining a mother's group who had formed because they all lost a child in the past few years. They would meet at someone's home each month to share an appetizer, a glass of wine and the repercussions of life after the loss of a child. At the first meeting, we went around the table and introduced ourselves, briefly sharing the circumstance from which our child died. The moms all knew each other intimately, and thoughtfully performed this exercise for my benefit and so I would feel welcomed. One by one, they spoke of car accidents and sudden illness and even suicide, and one by one, I felt the life sucked out of me again. They spoke calmly and rationally, and I felt like the only one totally out of control. I cried for their loss and their pain and took it all home with me that night. I couldn't benefit from the comfort they tried to extend to me, and couldn't separate myself from the pain I felt for them. Again, I never went back.

One particularly difficult and personal aspect of grieving which I found impossible to come to terms with was what happened to Steven's body from the train and what becomes of the body after death and before burial. The cold, rigor mortis experience was deeply embedded in my mind as my last contact with my once warm, energetic, affectionate child so full of life, his life so filled with potential. It made me physically sick at moments to think that my beloved son's body was basically slammed and crushed. The image of Steven in the casket still made my own body writhe with nausea and cramping. For this particular reason, I finally decided to seek out private grief counseling again so that I could somehow deal with these constant, debilitating thoughts, these horrific recurring nightmares preventing me from taking any genuine steps forward.

A family member of mine had been seeing a counselor for a specific life challenge he was facing, and I knew that he believed heart and soul in the ability of this man I'll call Alan, (because that's his real name). I decided to give Alan a try for a few reasons. First, I didn't want to keep "shopping" for a counselor and have to start at the beginning each time with the story of how Steven was killed. I knew that Alan had already been informed of some of the details of Steven's accident from our family member. Second, I tried private counseling again because I had come to the conclusion that I just wasn't comfortable in a group setting at that time. I needed a safe place to confide and vent and scream if I needed to, safely assured that no one else but a sole professional in a soundproof office would hear me. Finally, I chose Alan because I knew that he offered family therapy, and I knew how badly we all needed family grief support.

Alan didn't cry the first time I talked to him that summer. He wasn't silent, either. He gave me an opportunity to share my fears and put them in a little bigger picture to look at. He assured me that my nightmares would continue and that they were okay because it was the mind's way of working out what the consciousness of daytime suppressed. Alan sat quietly when I cried pure pain, and knew when to speak up, to challenge me to think beyond my irrational fears, which included something now happening to one of the girls. Alan remained objective and calm and helped me strategize through the waves of unsolicited advice and expectations and fifteen voice mails I received each day. Even the most mundane of worries, that I was woefully behind on thank-you cards or that I didn't return voice mails promptly enough were brought to their realistic level of low importance at that time. The first sessions of grief counseling I attended were full of tears. Chipping away at the details of the accident that killed Steven, the loss of our only son, the loss of our daughter's only brother, the absence of the boy "in the middle" of our family and our lives was often too much to verbalize.

Alan has now become a trusted friend — an older, wiser, objective friend. And I still see Alan today. He is now more of a life mentor to me, someone I can sit with and know I will receive honesty, whether I want to hear it that day or not, and somewhere I can still go to find a safe haven from the mixed-up world I now live in.

While my daughters only agreed to seeing Alan with me a few times, my own work with Alan gave me a better voice with my children, allowing me to be a more whole listener for them. I pray that I am also a more connected mother to my daughters, able to be better in touch with their needs. My husband sought out and found a counselor who was a father, a younger man who could relate to the unique feelings of loss Steve had for Steven. I feel good about my efforts with Alan in that they have not only benefited me, but ultimately my family and the way I communicate with them. Seeing the right person has allowed me to open myself up to be a true receiver, and to listen unguardedly, wanting honesty no matter what the cost, and without selectivity to hearing only what I want to hear. For this and so much more, I thank Alan.

I was sitting in the front pew at St. Patrick's Church, all the lights were on, and I was alone. I was staring blankly, envisioning Steven's casket in the aisle in front of the altar. I was extremely upset, reliving each moment of the accident, emergency room, wake and funeral.

Suddenly, Steven approached the pew and sat down next to me. He had a very worried look on his face. He said, "Mom, you have to stop this. I'm fine. Here, touch my arm. It's warm; it's soft. Touch my face. It's me. I'm not hurt, there's nothing wrong with me and I'm really, really happy."

I kept telling him that I just couldn't accept his death, that I couldn't accept this whole situation. He started to get mad at me then, telling me that I had to stop going over and over the details of his accident. He kept saying, "Mom, you have to stop this. Please, stop. Come on, do it for me."

I sat holding Steven in the pew for a long while, and finally felt contentment, at peace with the fears and visuals that had been shattering my every waking minute.

I woke up with my arms around my pillow. I thought of my work with Alan, and made a vow that very morning to stop focusing on the details of the accident over and over in my head, the coldness of Steven's body, to stop dwelling on the visions of the casket, to put an end to this self-torture. This is one of the gifts that the right grief counselor gave me, the freedom to let go of some of those dark thoughts and wake up to the light. *Yes, Lord, I know he's with You. He's safe and warm and living in eternity now. And he's really, really happy, like he said. Hey, I hope it's okay that I've chosen to keep a little part of Steven here, too. Good. I figured You'd be okay with that.*

* * *

PART II:
SEEKING OUT SYMBOLS AND SIGNS

CHAPTER 11: OF MOURNING AND MEMORIALS

I was able to derive new strength from my work in counseling. I felt physically stronger and more mentally focused during the day. I was finally able to keep some of those debilitating thoughts at bay. I was taking baby steps, now in the right direction, and no longer backwards. I silently held onto Steven, just as I had done in that dream. I didn't have to say good-bye to him as I thought was my only option. Feeling his spiritual presence guided my healing. I knew that I'd never again consider saying good-bye to this world, and to the family I loved so deeply. My life was changed, but not over. All of our lives were changed in different ways. We were four distinctly different people to Steven, and four distinctly different mourners as well. Although I was gaining strength and focus myself, my biggest job at home would be to try to help reconnect our family.

We definitely had a hard time supporting each other. This new family of four just couldn't reach each other yet. Grief counseling was closing some of those nightmarish doors for me, and opening new doors to becoming a better processor of my feelings, but I was light years away from being able to truly comfort my family in any measurable way. The mom who lost her only son couldn't reach out to the dad who no longer had his little boy. The older sister who was used to watching over her little brother couldn't comfort the little sister who missed her playmate. We were taking steps forward, but still walking around and past each other. We couldn't easily let go of who we were to Steven and to each other; meaningful interaction was a chore. At that time, we were frozen in a place where we truly wanted to stay; anytime before that fateful call on April 19, 2003. We didn't know who we'd become or how we'd get there. Grief is a long journey with little to no direction. We had fallen down, been stripped of some of our most defining roles, and needed to somehow rise up, take on new roles for one another, and try to do better than simply survive our injuries.

When I think of the girls at that time, I think of two innocent children standing on two cliffs, facing each other. They wanted to jump to the other side but couldn't. They were afraid to get too close to the edge because they would fall off. They'd look at one another across this black abyss, screaming for help but the other couldn't hear. The girls had such different personalities; Francesca such the quiet, first-born pleaser and Brianna the typical extroverted baby of the family, and the absence of their middle brother only accentuated their differences; the crater between them immeasurable. I didn't want to see a permanent gap form between these precious girls who now only numbered two through no fault of their own.

Where was the authenticity of our relationships with each other? Nothing seemed real, genuine. We were all caught in a stagnant place, failing to reconnect. I couldn't even bring myself to speak in terms of "older" child and "younger" child. Francesca was still my "oldest," Brianna my "youngest," the third gone but still in between. Whenever I bought them treats for occasions like Halloween, I still bought three of everything. I would just let them split the third. It would break my heart to not do or buy for Steven. Wasn't it okay to buy three Halloween treats?

I did divide up whatever we had saved for Steven's college education evenly between the girls. It made me sick to close those accounts. Why did we no longer have a third child to save for and plan with? Why, why, why? We thought and acted in terms of three because we didn't want to reduce our roles and relationships to a family of four with two children. This gaping, Grand Canyon sized hole was what lay over the cliff and what separated the girls. Too big. Too threatening. Too different. We needed to hang on to Steven but weren't hanging on to each other. How could we figure out how to do both?

We were one family grieving in four very different ways. My husband, for a long time, felt anger. He was angry with Steven for not being here, angry at himself for not being able to take him to his alma mater's baseball game that day which would have avoided Steven walking to McDonald's. Steve's grief counselor suggested that he purchase a toy train and take a baseball bat to it in our garage to release the anger he felt toward the train which killed our son. Steve wanted to take a bat to the real train, and no one blamed him. In our own unique ways, we all wanted to release our pent up feelings of revenge and rage, but my husband never took a bat to smash the toy train. The toy train lay motionless in the garage along with Steven's other toys — untouched. Revenge and rage? Still intact in all of us for a good long time.

Francesca seemed to harbor regret. Regret for not saying good-bye to her brother. Regret for not saying the things she would have said to him had she known he was going to die. Regret for all the helpless feelings you experience because you didn't realize what fate had in store for you. Up until that awful day, she only needed to be Steven's big sister. She shouldn't have needed to know or do anything differently than what she did. She had been a typical 8th grade girl with a somewhat annoying little brother who rode in the front of the bus with the other somewhat annoying fifth graders, and she made sure he got on and off the bus on time. Life was simple and predictable, and all it should have been at that age. How could she regret that she didn't prepare for what she didn't know was coming?

Brianna was filled with fear and anger. She was afraid of the train that killed her big brother. She feared the sounds of trains at night and the horns during the day. She worried that the trains would hurt someone else. And she was mad. Mad at the train, mad at what life handed her, mad that her protector and partner-in-crime was dashed away in a heartbeat, simply mad that she no longer had a brother. At the tender age of almost nine, my young daughter knew too well the cruelty of fate, and the helplessness of feeling like a victim. Nothing could easily fix this for her.

Combined with my feelings of self-blame and anger, we were quite the emotional cripples, the four of us. We wanted to move forward, but were paralyzed as a family unit. We wanted to jump across to the other side of the cliff to join the other, but feared another fall. So we stayed comfortably apart. If we swirled all of our extreme emotions and combined our forces, we'd have blown the roof off our house. Maybe that would've been better than the cordial distance we maintained.

I also quietly struggled with my rage toward the engineer of the freight train. I thought of his name day and night. We were told that moments before Steven's accident, the engineer was notified that two young boys were near the tracks and was told to slow down and sound his horn from a distance before that railroad crossing. I repeatedly thought of the details of Steven's accident, that any split second of timing would have prevented him from being struck by the cross train. I heard the engineer's name in my dreams. I pictured his face, although I never met him. I wondered if he knew how wonderful the little boy was that was slammed into a brick wall by his train, how much this boy was missed, how huge his unrealized potential. I begged to be forgiven for all the horrible fates my exhausted, sordid thoughts bestowed on this man. Then one day, I got a phone call. It was late afternoon, shortly before dinner, and I was halfheartedly trying to figure out what we'd eat that night. The phone call was from our attorney and friend who was gathering deposed reports on the train accident for us. There was no other way to obtain this sealed information and we needed to know every detail possible. It was the day that the engineer gave his deposition. I listened as our attorney told me how inconsolable the man was, how hard he cried and how could barely give his answers. I put the phone down and sat on the couch, bawling my eyes out, too. Knowing that the train engineer had such emotional feelings about Steven's death gave me affirmation that he was indeed a very real person who would probably be affected by the accident for the rest of his life. I knew that he felt remorse, and was sure that God forgave him. I prayed to God that I could, too, and felt the first shreds of my own remorse for questioning this man's conscience. Back then, I had a hard time forgiving anyone, mainly myself, so it didn't surprise me that I couldn't immediately process this new information and feel the forgiveness that I should have felt after the phone call. I wasn't yet my old self, thinking like my old self. The face in the mirror was still largely foreign to me.

It is said that life is on fast forward. This is true even in death. When mourning a death takes a back seat to the business of life, it is to everyone's detriment. Resurrecting our routines, trying to pick up the kids' needs at school and their extra-curricular activities came much too quickly, and didn't allow us the proper time to regroup, take a hard look at what happened to each of us, and try to reconnect in our new roles to each other. The process of grieving itself draws you together if you take the time to let it. Yes, life speeds too quickly ahead, even in times of extreme grief, if you don't stop and let the roof blow off the house. There was only time for remorse, regret and retaliation against inanimate objects. We needed to find each other again, but all of this "stuff" was in our way.

We couldn't heal as a unit, and we had little time to discern the situation as individuals. Schoolwork had to be made up. Teammates were looking for the kids to get back to their sports and dance. And again, we were also busily attending many thoughtful memorials throughout the month of May, which our school district had organized in Steven's honor.

There is no more comforting gesture than a memorial for your loved one to reassure you that others do not want to forget that person. At the same time, the events were so emotionally draining, so difficult to attend and keep our composure at, that we were filled with gratitude for those who organized these efforts but wrought with the pain of death at each one.

The first was little more than a week after Steven's death, when I received word that the Everett Elementary School Association of Parents and Teachers, called the "APT" at our district, donated several books about baseball players to our school library in Steven's honor. It was a series called, "The Baseball Adventure Series" by Dan Gutman, and featured books entitled, "Mickey and Me," "Shoeless Joe and Me," Jackie and Me," "Honus and Me," and "Babe and Me." Two dear friends of mine, Jenny Zinser and Peggy Schweller, had served as president and vice-president of the APT that year, respectively, so I wasn't surprised that they acted so quickly and generously to put this thoughtful gesture together. How Steven would love to know that other baseball loving students would be enjoying books about the most well-known legends of his favorite sport.

On May 15, the Deer Path Middle School Spring Chorus concert, entitled, "Sing Into Spring," was dedicated to Steven, and featured the most beautiful rendition of "I'll Be There," that favorite Jackson Five tune which Steven would surely be singing along to in heaven. We sat in the audience of the middle school auditorium that May evening, crying silently in the dark, parents filling rows of seats all around us, muffled cries amidst the songs. We couldn't fathom how the children were able to keep their composure so well, singing beautifully and with such warmth and spirit. We were touched at their kind gesture to remember their classmate who so loved this song.

One week later, the 5th grade spring concert featured a Swedish Folk Song called "Who Can Sail Without the Wind," dedicated and performed in Steven's memory. Everett School even named their annual outdoor games competition on the last day of school, Steven Malin Memorial Field Day. Again, we were speechless at the gestures.

Everett also dedicated their spring musical, "Hopes, Dreams and Wishes" to Steven's memory. The joyous voices of the young students, grades kindergarten through fourth grade, including Brianna's third grade class, surely brought happiness to their parents and the effort to bring comfort to us was another kindness beyond what we felt we deserved. Yet, as we sat in the folding chairs lining the Everett gym, all I could think about were the years that Steven himself participated in those very musicals. Now the musical was in remembrance of my dead son, and the spacious gym felt like it was sucking out my last breath. I sat next to my husband, swirls of emotion welling inside of me. No outlet, no one to catch the shards of grief exploding from me. This was our existence now, to accept the tributes, the kindnesses. Keep the composure, express the gratitude, and grieve quietly and alone. Never let the roof blow off in front of anyone.

I remember receiving a call toward the end of the school year telling me to come to the D.A.R.E. program awards presentation on June 3 at Deer Path Middle School. D.A.R.E. was a several week course, which Steven had taken that year along with the other fifth grade students promoting drug awareness, anti-drug philosophies and positive choices at the middle school age. I sat in the crowded bleachers at the Deer Path gym with other parents whose children were present and had been in the program with Steven. I was running late for the event after trying to get a few local errands done, and attended alone as my husband was at work. I had no idea that anything special was being planned in Steven's honor. I figured that the invitation was to make sure we felt included on the 5th grade end-of-year activities, nothing more. However, before our police department, who was in charge of the program, prepared to announce the winner of the 2003 D.A.R.E. Student of the Year, they called out to the audience to ask if "Mrs. Malin" was in attendance. I felt shaky as I meekly raised my hand from my seat. Our police chief then announced that the D.A.R.E. Student of the Year award was being changed to the "Steven Malin, Jr. Memorial Student of the Year Award" by the Lake Forest Police Department. The young 5th grade girl who came up to the podium to accept her award was all smiles. I was silently crumbling in the stands, again thankful for the deeply kind gesture from our police force, yet overcome with a flood of emotion, realizing that the word "memorial" would now forever accompany my son's name.

No time for self-examination to try to make sense of our new family dynamic, no real time for moments of transcendence to sort out our feelings in quiet. Immersed in attending memorials, getting our own kids to their activities again, we moved around each other, dancing around the true task at hand — our family's real mourning process. We weren't talking the difficult talks; we were keeping Steven's place at the dinner table empty rather than moving closer together. It's difficult to say you're really moving forward when you're not moving closer to one another. It's like walking apart toward the same battle line instead of forming an impenetrable wall for the enemy, which in our case was death. *Steven, we need your help, your direction, to help build our wall. Be with us.*

What none of us had the benefit of back then was time to sort out our destructive emotions and turn them into constructive words and actions. We were being comforted all around us but not comforting ourselves, or each other.

With the passage of time now, we've had many the difficult talks. I've had them with my husband, the girls have had them with each other, with Steve and me, and we've had them as a family. They've been painfully loud, and full of the screams we couldn't hear across the cliff tops back then. Yes, we've definitely blown the roof off our house more than a few times. And it really needed it.

* * *

CHAPTER 12: THE PROMISE — A RAINLESS RAINBOW

Of all the memorials for Steven those weeks, one of the events produced a miracle, and ended up being anything but sad. The memorial began as the others had, confirming what we thought was the permanent physical absence of our little boy. However, something happened at the end of it, which was so moving, so defining in our lives that I wrote an essay about the experience. What happened at this memorial set the stage for keeping Steven with our family, and also confirmed his life in heaven. It was our first "sign," the first time we looked up and knew Steven was just "overhead."

The essay was published in our local paper, and brought peace and affirmation to many in our community. Below is the original text, and the very reason I came to believe in "rainbows after the rain."

> *June 4, 2003, the last day of school before summer vacation, began as a cool, bright spring morning, but held sad significance for me. This day, I would attend the first annual memorial softball game played in honor of our 11-year old son, Steven, who was struck and killed by a train six weeks prior. Steven attended 5th grade at Deer Path Middle School in Lake Forest, and the co-ed softball game, organized by our Student Council, was one of several dedications generously made on Steven's behalf during the last weeks of school. How I wished he knew something of each thoughtfully dedicated event in his honor. How I hoped he could somehow look down on us and smile that infectious grin of his, and tell us all would be okay. Little did I know the powerful message this day*

would hold for me, and the turn my feelings would take because of it.

I knew that the softball game itself would be difficult to attend without Steven there, because our son ate, slept and worshipped the game of baseball. Sandwiched between two sisters, Steven was "all boy," as they say, enjoying a new sport as each season unfolded, but always particularly drawn to baseball. As I headed east on Deerpath Road, the scattered, high clouds in the blue sky mirrored my own thoughts, scattered between wanting to see his fifth grade class one more time before summer vacation, and the feeling of despair at the thought of trying to enjoy the games today without my favorite player there.

I arrived at the school baseball diamonds to the sounds of moms comparing and confirming the day's modified game rules, the kids' usual laughter and joking, and teachers rounding up their respective classes for the start of the first round of games. The rules of this special day of softball dictated that each of the two homerooms that played each game would get one "up to bat," comprising one big "inning," and while no "outs" were officially tallied, each game would be held to a time limit. This would not only ensure all classmates one turn at bat at each game, but the quick and efficient accumulation of runs in a shortened game.

After receiving hugs from many of the parents, and assorted high fives and hugs from the kids, I took a place behind the home plate fence. While I still felt my initial uneasy sadness at the day's event, it was soon replaced with an "energy" I could not describe. I, who had been so reluctant to partake in this one memorial, soon felt invigorated by the enthusiasm of the teams, alive from the smiles and cheers all around me. Indeed, the genuine joy emanating from these kids as the games began soon became contagious to all there. Especially me.

Many of the homeroom teams included boys who had played baseball with Steven over the years. They also included boys and girls who had been his friends since pre-school, or simply new friends he had made since attending Deer Path Middle. With familiar smiling faces everywhere, I felt privileged to cheer these kids on, to receive a "high five" from them as they drove in another run, or even made an "out." I cheered equally for each team, secretly thanking each of these kids for the immeasurable smile I proudly displayed honoring their efforts.

Through all the rotations of the morning games, one thing became increasingly clear. Steven's homeroom team, lead by their teacher, Mr. Ken Smith, calling themselves the "Sponges" as in "Sponge Bob," was determined to take the whole prize. It didn't hurt that the "Sponges" had the loudest cheerleaders, complete with posters that spelled out "S-m-i-t-h" as in Mr. Smith, their hero not only for his athleticism, but surely for getting them through the past month. This, I thought, was a serious team with a definite goal in mind.

I wasn't surprised to find that Mr. Smith's homeroom made it to the final championship game to be played after lunch. As I walked back to my car, making mental note of the time I had to be back for "the big game," I overheard a very excited classmate declare, "Steven is all around us today, don't you feel it?" Wish that he were right here, my friend, I thought as I pulled away.

Upon my return for this last, most important game, I felt none of the feelings I had early that morning. The contagious enthusiasm of these kids had enveloped me, and all I could think about was how happy Steven would be to see the last day of school celebrated this way. Many of the other homerooms were present for the championship and, including parents, numbered well over 100 spectators. The weather remained cool and pleasant, the sun and white clouds high in the sky, the temperature perfect.

Mr. Smith's team had "last ups," and the first worried faces appeared that day as Steven's homeroom realized that the opposing team had scored seven runs. As the first of Steven's classmates tensely began their turns at bat, I began to hear muffled shouts of "Maria, look up, kids, look up in the sky!!!" It was so noisy with the cheers of the game that it took me a few moments to understand what everyone was pointing to and yelling about. But there, up near the most beautiful, puffy white cloud emerged a streak of rainbow. It was not a semi-circle rainbow in the traditional sense, but a colored bolt of rainbow that hung solidly above the baseball diamond alone. As the kids jumped up and down and parents and teachers cried the tears of adults, I wouldn't know I was breathing except for my heart beating so hard in my chest. "It's Steven, it's Steven," the kids screamed, "he's here to make sure we win! Hi Steven!" they yelled as they stared and waved at the fluffy blue sky with the unexplainable rainbow pumping brighter and brighter. Could it really be you here, Steven? I miss you so much, is this you? I repeated this over and over in my head amidst a flood of tears. I couldn't clear my emotions enough in those moments to verbalize any of what I was feeling. We, as logical adults, struggle constantly with making sense of what we experience. Since losing my child, though, I had given up on logic, since logic could not explain why this horrendous accident happened to my gentle, funny, smart, wonderful boy. Instead, I was now seeking symbols. Signs and symbols of what I was now to grasp onto. Had I not witnessed this most powerful sign with 100 or so other stunned adults and children, I might never be able to retell the amazing story, or have outsiders believe me if I didn't have pictures of it as proof.

The colors of the rainbow brightened as each student took their turn for the "sponges," and each run added up to ten. Ten runs and much teamwork officially won the championship for Mr. Smith's and Steven's homeroom, with the rainbow streak protectively watching over the game and all who joyfully participated in it. Especially me.

As high fives and "good game" gestures were exchanged between the two teams, we stared at "Steven's Rainbow," as it was called that day, and watched it fade slowly, its message coming to a close much as the game was. As the kids walked back into the school and the parents gathered up the last of the equipment, the rainbow, too, shrank to nothing and disappeared. I still could barely speak at the power of what we all witnessed. Many of us stayed near our cars in the parking lot for a while and compared our feelings over what had just happened. Steven, who loved baseball more than anything in the world, was surely smiling down on us all, letting us know that all with him was indeed okay, and that we would be, too. Many slept more peacefully that night for the first time in weeks. Especially me.

* * *

CHAPTER 13: SEEKING OUT THE SIGNS

> *"Death is nothing at all. I have only slipped away into the next room. Whatever we were to each other, that we still are. Call me by my old familiar name. Speak to me in the easy way, which you always used. Put no difference in your tone. Wear no forced air of solemnity or sorrow. Laugh as we always laughed at the little jokes we enjoyed together. Let my name be ever the household word that it always was. Let it be spoken without effect, without the trace of a shadow on it. Life means all that it ever meant. There is unbroken continuity. Why should I be out of mind because I am out of sight? I am waiting for you, for an interval, somewhere very near, just around the corner. All is well."*
>
> *Henry Scot Holland*

So, if you choose not to say "good-bye," how do you keep the "hello's" coming? How do you hang on? Life after losing a child is filled with "truths." The obvious truth is that your "physical" child is gone forever. That physical, day-in, day-out connection is never going to happen again. But now I was sure I had to find us ways to hold Steven close to us forever.

Being from 100% Italian heritage, I came from a very "kissy" upbringing, and bestowed the same affection on my kids. I love to give my kids hugs. It was extremely painful as I missed hugging and kissing my eleven year-old son when he woke up in the morning, when he left for school, when he got home from school, before he went to bed at night, the spontaneous hugs in between, the endless opportunities to show my unconditional love for him and my daughters, as well. I can still smell the outdoor "boy" scent of his cheek, sometimes sweaty from playing sports, sometimes because, like many boys, he didn't scrub his face enough. It was all Steven, and now all physically lost.

Because I could not abandon that intense connection, I had to come up with some way in which my little boy would forever remain part of my daily existence. Many people tell me that they regularly talk to their deceased loved ones; that they keep near to them in a conversational way. This just wasn't enough for me. My constant conversation with Steven would amount to, "This is totally and completely absurd, buddy, don't you agree? Now come back and let's get to your second day of travel baseball tryouts, okay? Enough of this ridiculous nightmare."

Life is what you make of it, so I guess I needed to gather this new life, and in everyday terms, find our new means of communication with Steven. After the appearance of the rainbow at the memorial baseball game, I wanted to do anything I could to get another sign from him. If I lay in bed 24/7 with the covers over my head, which was pretty compelling in the beginning, I knew I'd never see signs from Steven, and he would be so unhappy that I chose this path of self-pity, dismissing the needs of our two daughters, giving up on living myself. Likewise, if I shrouded myself in this way, I'd never be open enough to receive him. But *how* to receive him? How could I receive the communication from my son that I so desperately needed? Rainbows weren't going to appear in the sky on a daily basis.

With many more years of parenting ahead of me, I had to figure out how I would embrace my two loving children here on earth, and still hang onto my child in heaven. Keeping all three children was now non-negotiable. I felt like Steven wouldn't have said "hello" through the rainbow if he didn't want to stay close to us as well. It was my job to keep my family of four as a whole unit, too. More steps, more risks to take, more opportunities to fall, but I'd now made a deal to see this through, no covers over my head. I finally realized that there was a vast world of difference between "going on" without Steven and simply "moving forward." I knew we all wanted to "hang on." I knew I had to move forward because I had two children who needed me to finish raising them. I had a husband who needed a functioning wife. I had countless responsibilities, most of which required me to put one foot in front of the other. "Going on," to me, meant letting go, forgetting some aspect of life before Steven died, leaving a past behind that could not be left. "Hanging on" was going to be our path, and looking for "Steven signs" all along the way would move us forward on it.

Taking those first real steps together, as a true family unit, were so very difficult. There is an endless list of "firsts" after you lose a child. First walk into the grocery store, first holidays, first birthdays, first outings, first vacation, the first time someone asks you how many children you have, first everything. The "order" of life which takes place when your child dies is unfair to say the least and unforgiving at best. First, you are given the shock and jolt of your lifetime, then you receive comfort, advice, and then you worry that everyone else has gone back to their usual lives but your family. So many of the firsts prove to be impossible. Impossible to take a first step, a first breath, a first look around this new world that still feels like it must be someone else's life, someone else's tragedy. Life is positively a walking landmine of "firsts" when your child has died, and ours was, as well.

Events and celebrations took on a completely new face without Steven. Brianna's ninth birthday was eight weeks after Steven was killed, and I remember us finding it impossible to "pose" for a family photo at her party without him. Why would we want a picture of our family of four? Even taking a simple photo seemed a waste of time. Who wanted to remember a birthday party without Steven there to sing? *Hey, Steven, could you give us some sign that you're here singing, too? That we just can't hear you?*

I thought long and hard about how I would manage to incorporate Steven into all the things in our lives which I knew still needed to happen on a daily, weekly, monthly or yearly calendar. Whether it was driving the kids somewhere, going to the mall, taking a family trip, or simply running errands, Steven needed to be a part of the framework of those efforts, a pattern in the design of the rest of our existence. We just could not move forward and leave him behind.

I will admit that the first "firsts" were the hardest: that first walk into the grocery store, that first dinner party with the neighbors, that first family party without him. I guess the seconds and thirds of those events weren't so easy, either. It is still hard. Every day is a new challenge in moving forward. The conscious decision to head out the door and continue life takes so much energy, energy that's been stripped away, from grieving, from crying, from insomnia that's zapped you of the last shreds of energy you thought you still had. But in the end, I now am so glad we chose to try. I feel strongly that because we tried and didn't give up, we found Steven's energy was there to help us.

Indeed, there is some guilt attached with the decision to move forward. It involves accepting and embracing happiness again. The hardest first steps to take were those that included any type of enjoyment, new memories, or heaven forbid, quality family time that didn't include Steven. How could I go out with my family to one of Steven's favorite restaurants without Steven? God help me that the first few times we did frequent a familiar restaurant and a waiter we knew would ask where Steven was. I felt so guilty even being there that I would stop dead in my tracks, have no idea how to answer the question, and want us to leave immediately. How could we dare go out for Japanese stir fry without Steven there to catch a piece of broccoli in his mouth? How could we go out for Greek food and not watch Steven devour a huge bowl of egg-lemon soup? How could we watch the end of a reality TV series when Steven saw the first episodes before he died and now wouldn't be there to see the final winner?

It seemed so unfair that Steven wouldn't see the winner of a TV show when we had no indication that he was leaving us, that he wouldn't see next week's episode. We could not attach "reason" in any shape or form to Steven's death, but we desperately still needed to somehow attach "purpose" to our lives as a family of four. But how?

The first times we headed out our door, just the four of us, usually began quietly. We all felt awkward and didn't say much to each other. It took one of us to loosen up the other three, and it usually seemed to amount to thinking of some memory, like Steven devouring Greek soup, or seeing some symbol that reminded us of him. And the symbols were pretty easy to find. They didn't have to be rainbows on a sunny day. The symbol could have been the Abercrombie kid's store at the mall, which Steven loved to frequent. It was sometimes as simple as seeing someone wearing a North Carolina basketball shirt, knowing it was one of Steven's favorite college teams, and we'd think of him and comment on it.

For others, seeing these reminders is nothing but pure pain. For us, we'd consider them a little "hello" from him that day while we were out, and they'd bring us such tremendous comfort. We also couldn't bear not talking of him, so Steven's name would be spoken at every family outing, whether it was commenting on how much he loved collared Abercrombie shirts or laugh at how he once caught the piece of broccoli in his mouth at the Japanese restaurant but almost fell over in his chair. And his name was spoken easily and "without effect, without the trace of a shadow on it." We would watch his favorite TV show and laugh at the familiar Six Flags commercial with the funny old man who Steven could imitate to a tee. To speak of and laugh about the Steven we knew kept him close on a daily basis. To remember that he liked his grilled chicken without any grill marks, that he ate the yolks of the egg instead of the whites, to compare his height to Brianna's at the same age felt easy and natural. We wouldn't let go; we'd hang on, and began to attach these memories and symbols to our daily lives. *We would consider the symbols that reminded us of Steven to be "signs" from him. Hi, Steven!*

It wasn't that hard to receive these signs, or to define them. Really, all we were doing was taking aspects of our everyday lives and remembering that many of them were part of Steven's life, too; his likes, dislikes, talents, struggles, personality traits and interests. Others may look at running into old memories as just that, and no more. We took it to the next level and considered them "signs" from the boy we so much wanted to hang onto, and sensing his nearness when we'd see a sign brought us respite. When I look back, the signs and symbols even happened in those first days; I just didn't realize it at the time. When we are closed, truly closed, to recognizing a message, a sign, a symbol, then we cannot receive it. It is that plain and simple. You must not only be thinking of your loved one, you must also be out in the real world. You cannot see anything with the covers over your head. "Moving forward" helped us run into Steven all the time.

* * *

CHAPTER 14: WE ALL HANG ON

We discovered that our close friends and family members hung onto Steven through their stories and memories of him. When we first received sympathy cards, we derived tremendous comfort from people who shared their favorite memories of our son and brother. We loved reading the cards because, like talking about Steven in everyday conversation and looking for symbols of him, it made him feel like a part of us still. I believe there is great healing in hearing your child's name spoken, reading a funny anecdote about him or her. The alternative route, not mentioning the name, the hush of death, is just utterly unbearable to me. We kept all the wonderful cards we received, more than 1,000 of them. I remember our mail carrier, Mark, finally commenting one afternoon as I took the mail from him that he never remembered delivering so many cards to one address in such a short time. I kept the cards and stories for more than the obvious reason. Of course, we wanted to keep the memories with us forever, but we also feared that we might forget something someone had shared with us. We wanted every memory preserved and safe. There was a teacher who shared a favorite conversation she had with Steven about his love of pasta with clams and mussels. There were coaches and dads who reflected on Steven's sportsmanship. There was our faithful friend, Sally Willis, who had observed Steven as altar server over the past year at St. Pat's, and shared their feelings of him serving that last Holy Thursday Mass two nights before he died.

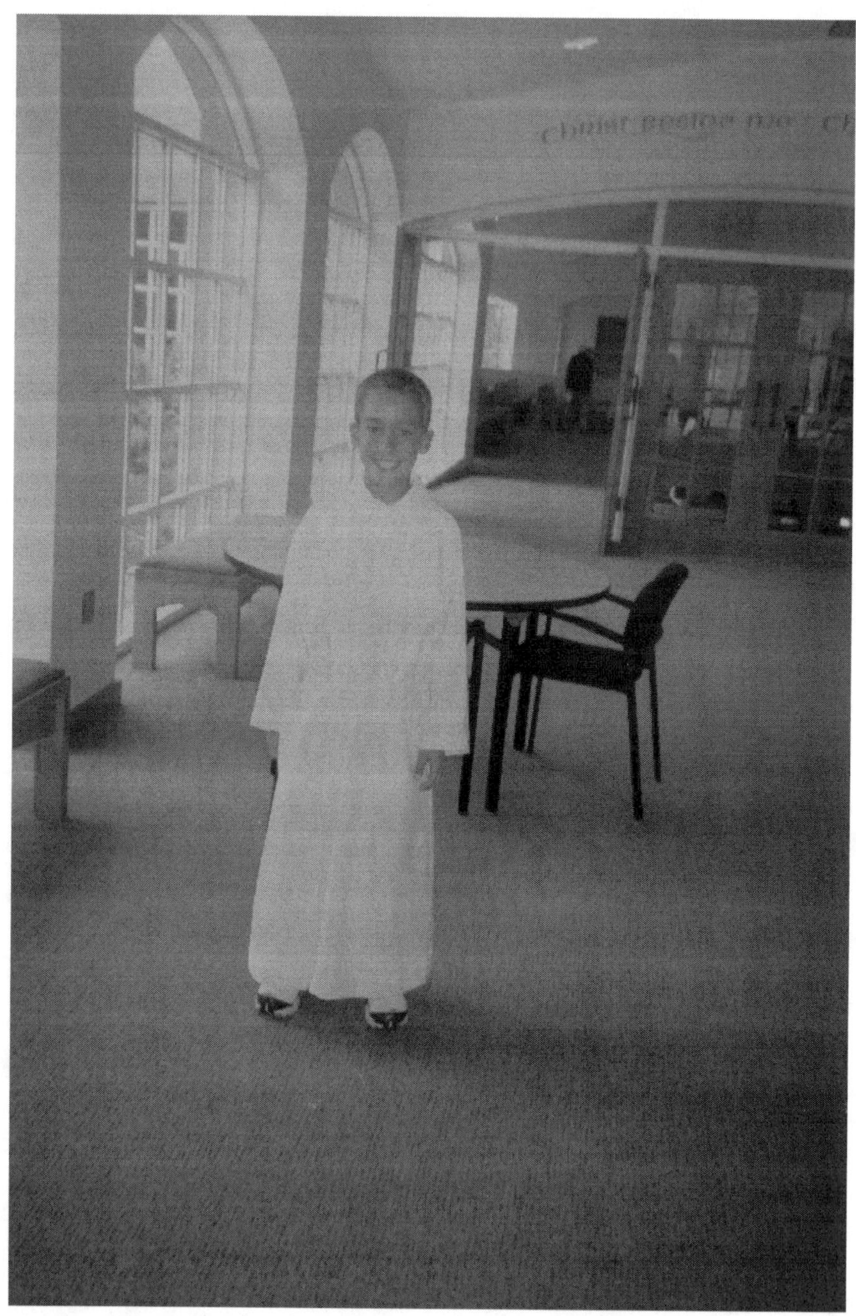

Steven in his altar server robe at St. Patrick's Church.

We felt such immense comfort in reading these messages that when Steven's school asked if there was anything the kids could do to help us, we asked the kids to send us their favorite "Steven story." Steven was fresh in all his friends' minds, and we had heard that many of the kids had been sharing their favorite memories of Steven with their parents and teachers anyway. We knew that we'd love to hear them as well, and so we made our request, and soon the funny stories began arriving from the classmates. We heard that Steven had a penchant for licking a spill, such as melted cheese from his nachos, right off his clothing at the school lunch table rather than going to the bathroom to wash it off (a maneuver he certainly wouldn't have tried in front of us).

We listened to tales of Steven and his buddy, Bobby Nommensen, leaving fake dog poop in the middle of a shopping mall and watching folks approach it, wondering if it was real, all while Steven and Bobby hid around the corner in a fit of hysterical laughter. We heard about fun in Spanish class with Signor Weinberg, and Steven's competitive streak during math games in Mrs. Binversie's class, and just a great and inside look at the regular, everyday life that Steven led that we wouldn't necessarily have heard about if he was here. Now, we had the chance to hear it all and keep it in our heart of memories. We didn't need to hear any superlatives about him to comfort us. We wanted to laugh and remember the regular child who lived a regular eleven year-old's life. We just needed Steven to stay close.

Some of the stories would have made us shake our heads had Steven been here to listen to them with us. But the truth was that now we didn't care about harmless mischief or sloppy manners at the lunch table. We loved hearing more about the little boy we missed so much and wanted to hang onto so badly. And these stories helped us hang on.

The first Christmas without Steven, some of our nieces and nephews got together and assembled a memory book of their favorite "Steven Christmas Stories." They included, of course, how many mounds of clams and mussels Steven could eat on Christmas Eve at his Aunt Diane's house, how fun it was to play hide-and-seek in the dark in the basement of Grandma and Papa's house on Christmas Day, how much potty humor could be amplified on an open microphone and a karaoke machine, and funniest-of-all, the enormous giggles when Steven placed a remote control under the dinner table during Christmas Eve which mimicked, um, "gastrointestinal sounds," and hit the button during the older adult's dinner conversation in the dining room. Hilariously enough, all these family members looked shockingly at each other at the seeming lack of propriety while all the little kids rolled on the floor in the next room in stitches, Steven repeatedly leading the release of the remote "gas" sounds.

I scrapbooked the stories of Steven, knowing that we would want to read them again and again, finding as many smiles as tears in re-reading everyone's favorite memories of this funny, heartwarming little boy who loved to laugh, and obviously make others laugh as well. I remembered a few of the many inspirational words of Maya Angelou, the great poet and author whose short lines of life wisdom continually spoke to me over this time. She says, "The main thing in one's own world is to laugh as much as you cry." Laugh we did. Cry we did, too. The tears, however shed, were filled with the water of life. His life. They didn't feel like the usual tears of death.

Indeed, we received so, so many accounts from Steven's life from those in our community, friends from school and sports, and even mere acquaintances that we could have compiled a mini-biography of our boy. They all shared their unique perspective on Steven from their respective relationships with him. The stories were as simple as those from moms like our dear friend Geri Galassini, who told us of the hugs she'd steal from Steven in the hallways at school if she was there volunteering or dropping off a forgotten lunch. There were folks from our community whom we really didn't know personally, like the Lyons family of Lake Forest, who sent us a few photos and words remembering a hot summer day when Steven and Brianna, then very little and dressed in red, white and blue, stood next to her kids, by chance, at a summer parade. People came out of the woodwork, taking the time to share one instance or one hundred instances where their lives met his. Yes, from the moment of Steven's death, those around us reached out in monumental ways to share memories and help us not say good-bye to him or our life with him.

And as with anything, there were also those folks who offered their "insight" on remembering lost loved ones, and it wasn't advice we needed or wanted to hear. I had the displeasure of talking with an old family friend at a graduation party shortly after Steven left us, who shared the story of the loss of her nephew and how her sister coped. She patted my hand, looked me square in the eye and said, "Don't worry, you'll never forget Steven." At that very moment, I wanted to take her hand and slap her own face with it. Reassure me that I wouldn't forget my own son? She had to be out of her mind. I felt out of my mind listening to such garbage, was brave enough to walk away from the conversation, and am now smart enough to stay away from her each time our paths cross at an extended family function.

Yes, "moving forward" is absolutely necessary. Doing it alone doesn't have to happen. Although no one could change the fate of April 19, 2003, the people who formed such a protective bond around us helped so much. No, they couldn't have helped Steven hear the oncoming train. They couldn't have changed one second of the timing, which caused our ultimate disaster from occurring. What they did do and continue to do is help us move forward by "hanging on" with us. We received hundreds upon hundreds of messages that said, in essence, "If we could take one ounce of this burden off of your shoulders and place it on ours, we would." That repeated offer of sharing our burden was so immensely touching to us that I still can't even put its meaning into written or spoken words. While the journey seems impossible in the loss of a child, just knowing that you're not going through it alone makes it more bearable. Taking moments of peace on this endless journey to smile and laugh about your child with someone who knew him and wants to keep his spirit alive with you helps you carry the load a little further, a little longer. I have often said that I don't need to meet anyone new in my life; I'm content with only having those around me who knew Steven. I selfishly want to preserve as much of my life before Steven died as possible, and although I can finally move forward with meeting new people, I absolutely cherish those in my life who also knew him. It is those people who help keep his spirit alive, who knew us pre-April 19, 2003. The journey of life since that date is no shorter. The journey without our child is as long as the rest of our own lives, but having special friends and an unbelievably caring family around who help us hang on and move forward means that there's a light shining on the path that makes this long, tiring journey not so dark at every bend. It's also what makes us feel like Steven is on the journey with us, guiding our way, infusing his strength into our next step forward.

If I could make one recommendation to anyone who is trying to comfort another parent who's lost a child, someone who's lost a sibling, or just anyone who is grieving over the loss of a significant loved one, it's this: *Don't forget.* In fact, do any thoughtful thing you can do to show them that *you* remember their loved one. Since losing my son, I regularly call those who have also experienced significant loss on that loved one's birthday, anniversary, or any other milestone just to leave a voice mail that says, "Hey, I'm thinking of you today and remembering so-and-so on their birthday." Or, on the anniversary of the death, which is always, always a horrible day, I'll send a card or email that might simply say, "I know this is a hard day for you, you're in my thoughts and at the top of my prayer list today." Even though that grieving person may seem like they slide through the milestones without much mention or emotion, let them know that *you remember.* We'll receive notes in our mailbox, or a bunch of flowers, even a Mass card on those days. We may just get a voice mail or email saying that a friend is thinking of us on the day of Steven's death, what we now call "his birthday in heaven." As Christians, we believe that when our loved ones go to the Lord, they begin eternal life. So, we now quantify these years by calling them Steven's "birthdays in heaven." It's just what we've coined it. Like the rest of this, we've made up our own rules to get along; our journey, our steps, our rules. "Birthdays in heaven" are one of those rules. We don't want Steven to stop having birthdays, especially since he now celebrates at the right hand of God.

I have been so deeply appreciative of gestures of remembrance at Steven's birthday or anniversary of his death, or even what would have been his 8th grade graduation, that my family and I can better get through those days simply because we feel the love and presence of someone who is especially thinking of us that day. "Presents" are not needed on those occasions, but "presence" is. If you are in the position to help someone who's grieving, let your "presence" take the form of however you think it would be best received. If you want to show up with a hug, do so. Maybe a simple email would suffice. You know the person, and you hopefully would know the best approach. But don't be afraid. I have spoken to so, so many folks who agree on the healing powers of letting those in grief know that they are not alone on their journey, that you are there with them in whatever shape or form, for the duration. That you remember. That you want to help them hang on to the good stuff. Letting go is too hard. Saying good-bye doesn't have to happen.

So, don't let the grieving loved one in your life walk their path alone. Don't just be there for the wake and the funeral or to visit once or twice. At the holidays, think of them with a special card or even a special note inside their normal holiday card. To many in serious grief situations, the holidays can be the saddest time of the year.

After receiving so many poignant sympathy cards that spoke beyond the grave and death, I personally now make a point of giving sympathy cards which send the message of "life journey," and "journey after life." The journey "to heaven" if one is a Christian. The journey "from this life" if one is another religion that does not believe in the afterlife. Not finality, good-bye forever, but a path. I am on a path, with many, many good friends and family members who help us remember and keep Steven with us. And boy, is he with us.

* * *

CHAPTER 15: HE IS HERE WITH A HALO

As I said, so many people had sent dinners, breakfasts, baked goods, flowers, books, inspirational gifts, religious icons, cards, letters, mass intentions. The list was endless, the volume so overwhelming. We were speechless at the outpouring of care. Friends and family extended us lifelines from every direction, in every category of kindness imaginable. With such constant support, we were fed — literally and figuratively. Once we began to truly process all the support shown to our family, we thought long and hard over how we could possibly show our gratitude. Gratitude. Now there's a word. That deep, alive feeling of wanting to connect back with so many who fed us life when we thought we'd surely drown alone. I didn't know how we'd find an appropriate way to show our gratitude. I could be writing thank-you cards forever. The thought of over 1,000 handwritten cards was daunting. Still, I could not ignore the sincere outreach from family, friends, our community, even those we didn't know, and would find a way to express our feelings to them all. My sister, Diane, and sister-in-law, Rose Marie, immediately stepped in, their assistance always a phone call away, offering endless help in organizing all of the people we needed to thank. They created databases. They organized the gifts. They were a steady presence in so many, many tasks that were impossible for me to tackle alone over those months.

Because of my love of writing, I began to draft a thank-you from our family that could be printed in quantity, but would still reflect our personal sentiments. I would scan in our last family photo at the top of the one-page sheet, the five of us smiling, ready to leave on a two-hour dolphin-watching excursion in Marco Island, Florida, just two weeks before Steven's accident.

The backdrop of the stationery was a beautiful sunset, and it reminded me of the peaceful feeling I had on that trip. I included the photo partly because I knew it was the last time I would be sending out a "real" family picture, that of the five of us, and partly because it was such a cute picture of Steven, suited up in his Hawaiian style swim trunks and life jacket, safe in our care, happy to be off to a little family adventure in Florida. Our family looked tanned and rested, having just enjoyed a wonderful spring break vacation. Our daughters looked pretty and carefree, their smiles eagerly awaiting an afternoon of dolphin watching and fast waverunners. Under the photo would read: *"It doesn't matter how long we live, but how we live and how we love that counts."* I received this quote from a young woman, a family friend named Katie Apfelbach, who baby-sat for the kids over the years, and had included this quote in a wonderfully heartfelt letter she sent to us after Steven's death. The quote stuck with me because it echoed the famous quote of Abraham

Lincoln's, which says, "And in the end, it's not the years in your life but the life in your years."

I thought long and hard about the words to the body of the letter. I wanted it to be thoughtful and thorough, but not ten pages long. So many people had done so much for us and I could have gone on and on. But it needed to be one page. So the letter read:

> *It is hard to begin to say "thank you" when those words seem inadequate to express how we feel. The outpouring of love and support we have received has helped us know that we are not alone.*
>
> *If you prayed for us, we heard you. If you hugged us, we knew you were trying to give us your strength. Your words of comfort told us that you care. If you shared a memory of Steven, it made us smile. The abundant food and flowers sent reminded us of life and how it must continue.*
>
> *If you made a donation to Lake Forest Parks and Recreation, know that we are committed to implementing an improvement that will benefit the numerous children who enjoy Lake Forest parks and facilities. If you made a donation to your own cause, we thank you equally.*
>
> *We have heard many times now that time may never lessen our pain. We hope, however, that love and faith will. We believe that Steven will someday greet us all again in heaven with his signature "smasher" hug. Until then, we will somehow rebuild the happiness of our "physical" family of four, and know that, in our hearts, we are forever five.*
>
> *With every ounce of thanks we can give, please know how much we appreciate everything you have done to show your concern for our family.*

> *We understand that Steven's last word was... "Perfect." That is how he viewed many things in his life. Not because they truly were, but because that is how he saw them. "Perfect" ranked right up there with "Yessss" and the ever-popular "Sweeeet."*

Although I revised it many times, I think that the final draft of our thank you letter said what I thought our family wanted to say. The trouble was the closing. I personally never liked the thank-you cards I'd receive from the loved ones of someone who died where they'd just sign, "The family of John Smith." If I were John Smith, I think I'd want to be on the card, too. After all, the effort was for me. Signing our thank-you letter was a difficult task, and I think I spent more time on the signature line than I did on the body of the entire letter. It would be the first time we would send something as a family that required our signature. How to do it? How would I maintain the integrity of the family of five that I so desperately wanted to preserve, and still acknowledge the fact that one of us was no longer physically here? How would I face a life of signing countless birthday, graduation, Mother's Day, Father's Day and other cards without Steven's name on them? This dilemma, like so many others, hit me smack in the face. There never seemed to be an end to navigating life without your loved one. The simple exercise of signing the card had become excruciatingly difficult that afternoon, and I considered my choices as I stared at the draft of the thank-you letter. Should we, too, follow protocol and become "the family of Steven Malin?" This just felt awful. But how could letting go of one of your children ever feel anything but awful?

I finally came upon an idea that would work for me, and one that I know would please Steven if he had a chance to express his opinion on the topic. I typed this last, most important line and added a "magic touch" above Steven's name, which would become the symbol of our family, our faith in Steven's new life with God, and a commitment that he still holds a most treasured place in our family of five, and always will. I smiled as I artfully added a swirled "halo" over Steven's name.

In having Steven's name on our thank-you card signature, I felt good knowing that Steven would be part of our sentiments. However, because it is my nature to worry about everything in life, I also wondered what folks would think of the "halo signature." Would they think I was crazy? Would I be viewed as being out of touch with reality? Would people say I had not accepted my son's death? (And *who* here wants to simply "accept" death?) But as the feedback came in over that first thank-you card, I, as usual, had worried over nothing. The feedback was positive, life affirming, in line with our philosophy that although a child has died, they are and will always be a member of their family, forever deserving of a signature on a card. Forever worthy of a halo, in my mind. Angels are angels forever, right? The halo, itself, was also a confirmation that Steven lives on with God. Although I still struggled with the hand that God had dealt us, I knew that Steven deserved nothing less than to be in God's special room for little angels, even angels who had mastered a bit of mischief. And I knew he was there. Keeping him with our family signature keeps him close to us here as well.

One of the most hope-inspiring aspects of the decision to sign Steven's name with the halo is the fact that others now address cards and such to our family with Steven's name and the precious halo over it. They, too, found it just as difficult to address a card simply to Steve, Maria, Francesca and Brianna Malin, with Steven, Jr. clearly missing. We are not, nor ever will be, "The family of Steven Malin." We are five who are joined in life and have chosen to stay five even through death. We use the halo for every Christmas card and for special greeting cards we send, and keep Steven close by doing so. Of course, we keep the halo signature for our dear family and loved ones, for those who knew Steven, for those who understand our need to keep his name with ours. Are there times when I simply sign, "The Malin Family?" Of course. There are definitely times when we know it is more appropriate to a specific situation to not sign Steven's name. Maybe we don't know the recipient of our card well enough to sign his name, or maybe that person didn't even know there once was a "Steven" in our lives, and so we don't do it in those cases. But mostly, we choose to include our little boy with the halo we swirl over his name, forever nestled between the names of our family. Right where he should be. Forever.

Expressing our gratitude to all of these special people actually reincorporated gratitude itself back into my daily life. At that time, I made a small, quiet, personal promise that I would live each day including three gratitude elements in it. First, I committed to finding something to be thankful for each and every day. Granted, I couldn't muster up ten things at that time, holding myself to just one for starters. Second, I counted one blessing every day. Usually, these were times that I saw my girls making headway as they began their healing journey, and I'd stop and reflect on it. Finally, I looked for someone each day who carried a bigger "cross" than me. And you know what? They weren't as hard to find as I thought. Amidst the rubble of thinking that you have experienced the worst devastation known to man, there are people suffering as much if not more than you in their own lives. Indeed, kindness shown to us led to gratitude back to others, in turn leading me to seek out moments of thankfulness and blessings. Simple math, huh? Keeping Steven along in those moments of reflection made them nothing less than profound. Today, I count many blessings every single day again. And the more I moved forward on this small, quiet personal journey, the easier the math got.

To the living, I am gone.
To the sorrowful, I will never return.
To the angry, I was cheated out of life.
But to the happy, I am at peace.
And to the faithful, I have never left.
And to those who choose to keep me close, I am right here.

Author Unknown

* * *

CHAPTER 16: ATTACHING MEANING TO MOTIONS

Seeking out the signs and symbols that reminded us of Steven proved to begin a real process of healing for our family as a whole, leading us to a genuinely better place than where we'd been. Whereas the separation process of death was a complete failure, the signs from Steven began to give us hope that we really didn't have to be "separated" from him. We could find him any day, any minute if we just looked for something that reminded us of him. This caused us to look back at events, even from the day of his accident, with new insight and meaning. Connecting the meanings also allowed us to revisit extremely painful days and weeks with some measure of clarity. We wanted to start digging out, so we started back at the beginning of this blurry journey.

As I reflect on the first days after Steven was killed, I can't pinpoint how or why I did what I did. There was no time to plan, to think, to strategize. I was fragmented, out of my own body, moving and doing without direction. I felt no inner self. I sat at a cold, stoic funeral home on Easter morning, and when we were asked who might receive any monetary donations in Steven's name, I suggested maybe our park district — a purely spontaneous decision based on the fact that our kids had enjoyed so many programs there over the years. In the end, because of such generous donations of money and assistance, a much-needed baseball field was renovated, dedicated in our son's name and donated to our town. Less than forty-eight hours after Steven left us, my husband and I visited our son's classroom to offer our support for what the children were going through. Purchasing the poster board and supplies at Office Max, and buying extra for the fifth graders to get involved and help celebrate Steven's life lacked any premeditation. The idea came to me out of nowhere. Knowing that I was in no shape to be making conscious efforts those first days, I know there had to be a stronger presence guiding my actions. In my mind, there is no doubt that it was Steven holding the strong hand of God, and God guiding my actions. *Lord, were you there all along? Why didn't I feel it?*

The Friday after the funeral, my husband and I drove to order a cake for our daughter's belated Confirmation dinner, a small family dinner at a nearby restaurant that we decided to still host for her despite the horrific week we had all experienced. Francesca so deserved our acknowledgement and blessings on the special occasion of her Confirmation, so we headed to the local bakery to pick out a simple cake. We questioned ourselves as to whether it was appropriate to have cake so soon after burying our little boy. We felt so guilty at the thought of anything celebratory. In those first days of shock, you wonder and question everything, and we discussed the decision on the way to the bakery. During this conversation, what song came on the radio but the Jackson Five song we had played at Steven's funeral. "I'll Be There," which hardly ever came up on the stations we listened to, shocked my husband and me to such a degree that we sat frozen in the car, crying hysterically. We looked at each other and wondered what the meaning could be to hearing the song at that very moment. Looking back, I now know it was a sign from Steven letting us know that indeed, Francesca should have cake at her Confirmation dinner that Sunday.

Later on that same day, my husband went to the gas station to fill up our tank, and when he was done, approached the car with a stunned look on his face. He said that as he waited in line to pay the cashier, he stared at a case of packaged hot dog buns near the register. As he remembered how much his little buddy loved hot dogs, one of the packages fell off its stack and onto the floor. A sign from Steven? A "hello" to his dad? As we remembered the incident, suddenly we were open to the possibility that the package of hot dog buns fell for a reason, and now think of it as Steven again reaching out to his dad that day.

In hindsight, even the nightly thunderstorms, blanketing our town the first week or so after Steven's death, were a sign. Were they a sign of the turmoil from above at letting one of earth's promising young lives come to such an abrupt end? Was the rain a sign from Steven acknowledging the water of our constant tears? Today, I believe that the rains came as a precursor to the rainbows that followed. During those black days, the violent weather only made me feel that much more upset and out of control. Today, I see storms with the hope of seeing sunshine afterwards, of witnessing a rainbow. I see rainbows as signs from Steven that God keeps His covenant; that Steven is indeed with our Lord. I think that the heavy and dramatic rains were the preparation we needed to make sure that we sought out and appreciated the symbolism and color of the rainbows.

One of the many, many days I stayed in the house those first weeks of spring, I would dread summer coming. I wanted the rain to stay, the gloomy weather to continue to mirror my solemn state. One day, I found myself looking out onto our back patio, remembering fun outdoor parties at our home from prior summers, wondering how they would ever happen again. Once when we had a few families over to cook out, our friend's daughter, Kelsey Kleinert, along with our two daughters, took Steven and another little friend named Kevin Tosi, and dressed them up in their dance recital costumes, complete with hair bows and make-up.

Steven, ever the performer, posed for many "photo ops" that day. As I stood there daydreaming, reminiscing about these happy times, I swear that I began to smell a barbecue. I followed the strange smell into our family room, and it got stronger near a set of family photos on an end table. I will say that it was a windy day, but no doors or windows were open to my knowledge. Maybe this sounds like the crazed delusions of a mother in the throws of extreme grief, but that day, it wasn't to me. I now take it as simply one of many signs from our son, wanting to let us know that our family memories would forever be there, and that day, exactly where to find them. I stared at the photos on the end table, photos of a laughing, close family, enjoying much more than a summer barbecue. Our family of five enjoyed life in general, and no one could take that away from us. I stood and cried the familiar tears of longing for that old life back. But I also thanked Steven for giving me a sign when I so needed it. I was just glad that my eyes were open to seeing it, er, smelling it. To this day, I have no real explanation of where that smell came from. I can only be thankful that I was open to it, and that this Steven moment gave me such comfort.

I remember one of the first times that Francesca received a sign from her little brother, shortly after his death. She was under so much stress at school trying to catch up on her schoolwork, trying to keep some semblance of concentration as she completed her eighth grade year and approached graduation. Math had been a challenge that year, and she worried about an upcoming cumulative test shortly after returning to school. I waited pensively for her after school when I would hear of how she did. My husband was coming home from work and had also been expressing worry over the pressure on our sweet girl, and how much losing Steven had taken its toll on both of our daughters. I was relieved to hear the news that she had done well on the math exam, but her real joy came in telling her dad. The joy wasn't only about earning an "A" on the test, but that while telling Steve the good news as he drove in his car, he looked up and saw a sign — literally a "sign." As Frankie told her dad the good news of her math grade, Steve saw a restaurant's sign from the car windshield. What other name could the restaurant be called but, "Steven's Restaurant." Steve and I attributed the restaurant sign as Francesca's first real "sign." I hadn't heard that joy in her voice since the day before she lost her little brother.

One night, my husband and I were in Steven's bedroom looking at some of his things, his room exactly the same as the day he left it months before. We were both extremely upset, still not registering the permanence of the loss, still begging that somehow this was all temporary. That evening in our son's room, my husband reminisced about passing Steven's bedroom in the early morning hours as he left for work, Steven laying on his stomach in bed, chin propped in his hands, secretly catching a few hours of ESPN before the rest of the house woke up and caught him playing a little "sports hooky." Stevie's canned response was always, "Hey Dad, don't tell Mom on me." We laughed between our tears, as usual finding it difficult to share any story or memory of our son that didn't make us smile between the emotions. Just then, my husband sat down on Steven's bed, in the very spot where our little guy enjoyed his ESPN catch-ups. My husband jumped up as that spot on Steven's bed was warm, unexplainably warm to the touch. Where did that come from? We both felt shaky as we tried to grasp on to this, another strange and unpredictable occurrence out of the blue. But then, just as suddenly as my husband shot up, we both quietly embraced the moment. We placed our hands over the spot on the bed and kept them there till it cooled. It was a few moments of peace, of enjoying what became labeled as another sign from Steven. And we definitely were open to anything that would keep our little boy in our world, no matter where or how.

"1032." It was the time of night that Steven was born. 10:32 p.m. on January 20, 1992. We often joked about the time because as we were in the delivery room and I was pushing, I would tease my husband that he caught the end of his favorite 10:00 nightly episode of the "MASH" TV show, and then came around the bed to hold my hand while I delivered our son. I would joke to everyone that my husband's favorite show ended at 10:28, and he gave me his utmost attention and support for exactly four minutes. Regardless of the lightheartedness attributed to the time in which Steven entered this world, I will be forever in awe of the symbolism of 10:32 since he left this world.

We found the piece of property in which to build our new home in Lake Forest when our younger daughter, Brianna and I drove past a "for sale" sign whose phone number ended in, what else, the number "-1032."

Our older daughter has repeatedly told me of looking at clocks in high school, in her car, and now in college when the time reads 10:32. She is not thinking of the time, hoping to catch a clock at that time, or placing any other focus on a clock or watch, other than accidentally finding it to read "10:32."

Frankie recently called with another most baffling experience with this number. She phoned from college complaining that her watch was intermittently stopping and starting, wondering what the cause could be. I suggested that if it was the watch battery, that her watch would be more apt to be slowing down rather than stopping and starting. After talking about this curious occurrence for a few minutes, I jokingly told her that if her watch stopped at 10:32, this would truly be something to report. I got a frantic phone call the next morning from a breathless daughter. The watch had stopped during her morning class. The time? 10:32, of course. She took out her camera phone and captured the moment, and spent the remainder of her day enjoying this sign from Steven.

Were these more messages from Steven? Was he trying to make sure we knew that he was connected to us? We believe so, heart and soul. And again, if we weren't looking, seeking out these signs, we wouldn't find them. We wouldn't attribute a failing watch to anything but a failing watch. The signs didn't jump out at us or come find us as we hid under the blanket of our bed. We were consciously attributing symbols to our son and brother, looking to make connections, hoping that they'd continue to unexpectedly pop into our day. We wanted there to be signs, so we kept looking. And we still do today. And we will forever.

Some of my mom friends decided that it was a good idea for us to form a walking group together. I knew that they were trying to get me out of the house and thought that the mixture of normal conversation and fresh air would do me good. I would meet them at one of their houses, and we'd walk a few miles down toward the Lake Michigan beach where we live. One particularly beautiful sunny morning, we met in downtown Lake Forest to head down toward the lake. I hesitated to go that morning because that day's route meant that we had to walk across a set of railroad tracks; not the tracks where Steven was killed, but a set of tracks nonetheless. As I walked gingerly across the railroad crossing, knowing that my dear friends were by my side, I looked down. Wedged in the railroad tie was an open pack of Mentos candy. My son always asked for Mentos whenever a treat was purchased at the store, and I found it unfathomable that of anything to be caught in those tracks, it was Steven's favorite candy! I didn't pick it up at first because I was in a bit of shock and wanted to get across the tracks as quickly as possible. As I shared the coincidence with my friend, Pam Kleinert, on the way down to the beach, she urged me to pick up the candy on the way back. I, who was so afraid to cross the tracks to begin with, couldn't wait to get back to find the Mentos roll, what I now consider a sign from Steven. Luckily, they were still there when we returned, and I still have them today. My sweet little boy was there with me, letting me find his favorite sweets, telling me from above that it was okay to cross the tracks and that he was close.

We discussed the "signs" with our family and closest friends. We told them of the coincidences from the first days after the accident. We explained how comforting it was for us to look for things in our everyday life that reminded us of Steven, and label them as signs. Soon, they began to look for symbols as well. They would hear songs on the radio that reminded them of Steven, look at them as a "hello" from above, and call to tell us about them. They all knew about the miraculous sign of the rainbow at the baseball field. Our friends and family all began to feel hope after the most hopeless months we had ever experienced. Steven felt close, just around the corner. We weren't saying good-bye. We were finding new ways to say "hello" to him.

My sister, Diane, who kept such a close and comforting eye on our family, called up one morning with news of a sign from Steven. She had been making breakfast for her own family of five and, feeling scattered and distracted herself at that time, left buttermilk biscuits in the oven far too long. She had forgotten to set the timer, and was afraid to open the oven door for fear of the charred remnants that surely remained, having been disastrously burned on the cookie sheet. Instead, after all that time, what she found were a dozen perfectly baked, lightly browned biscuits, just waiting for her three children to enjoy. Diane remembered that Steven loved buttermilk biscuits, and was sure that he wouldn't have wanted those to be ruined for her family.

In general, it meant so much to us, and everyone around us, that we all still had Steven's daily presence in our lives. We knew that we had to look for the signs, open our eyes and open ourselves up to receiving them. We had to attach meaning to everyday happenings that didn't demand meaning. We chose to attribute their meaning as signs from Steven. And we knew that they weren't going to come unless we looked for them.

* * *

CHAPTER 17: SIGNS FOR ME ALONE

There were times that I felt like Steven's signs were meant for me alone. And sometimes I needed them to be just for me. It was like continuing the special mother/son bond that I'd been so fortunate to have with him. The signs felt like "our little secrets." I could keep them like I had kept inside jokes between us when he was alive. We had shared a similar sense of humor, laughing at the same silly things, perfecting imitations of TV and movie personalities and assorted foreign accents, wondering why we "got it" and the rest of the world didn't appreciate how witty we were. I deeply missed that part of my everyday life, and that connection to Steven in it. So, it was no wonder that I felt a few of his signs were mine to keep for myself. Sometimes a sign was in the form of a dream about Steven, a visitation of a son to his mom.

The fall of 2003 found me occasionally driving Francesca, then a high school freshman, home from the Lake Bluff Golf Course after her golf team practices. The course was near our home, and she had tried out for golf for her freshman fall sport, making JV cheerleading for the winter season. I would regularly pass a park on Green Bay Road near the course, and would often see a local youth football team running from school at Green Bay and Illinois Roads to West Park, as it's called, for their daily practices.

That fall, I had a dream that when I drove past West Park, I saw a football team of young boys sitting in Purdue uniforms listening to their coach. Purdue was a favorite college team of Steven's. I kept looking for Steven among the football players. Where was he? Why wasn't he here to enjoy his fall football season? As I combed through the players in their helmets, one of them turned and took his helmet off. Silently, the player looked at me and slowly showed the biggest, most beautiful smile, which I recognized instantly. It was Steven, of course, and he stared at me in silence with that shining grin of his. I wanted to run to him but knew I couldn't physically reach him now. After a few long moments of comforting eye contact with me, he nodded and replaced his helmet. He returned his attention to the coach, and I drove off. I knew he was among those players. He was there all along; I just didn't know it till that day.

One of the signs came during late fall of 2004, on a sunny, unseasonably warm afternoon. We had been renting a house for six months after moving away from our old home near the scene of the accident, awaiting the completion of the new house we were building in another section of town. The rental home was small but clean, and with a finished and empty basement, kept us from having to place any of our valued possessions into storage. I was leaving the rental house to run a few homebuilding errands when the sight of a large Autumn Maple tree in the front yard stopped me cold. The tree had lost all of its leaves; all but two. There, waiting on the bare tree, hoping for me to see them were two perfectly shaped, red Maple leaves, one for Steven and one for me. My son knew that my favorite color in the whole world was red, and the two vibrant red leaves amidst all the barren branches was a sign of our connection, a sign for me alone. Amongst all the empty branches there would always be the two of us. Mother and son forever.

That fall in the rental home, I had reluctantly sent out Steven's bedroom set for refinishing. We had first purchased it when he was two and just out of the crib, and the wood finish didn't withstand the constant torture of water glass rings, magic marker stains, numerous scratches and other assorted love scuffs from our son. It was also a bleached oak, and my intent was to create a new bedroom in our new home, more masculine with darker woods, not a duplicate of Steven's old bedroom, but a new and simple guest bedroom. There would be other spaces in the new home dedicated to Steven, but we would not try to create his exact bedroom again. I contemplated whether I should touch his set at all, leaving his marks on it as more evidence of this typical little boy who treated his bedroom set in typical little boy fashion. At the time, I thought that refinishing the set and darkening the stain would have been what I would do for him had he still been here, getting older and ready for a more teenage look, so I thought I should still go ahead with the work.

I had been worried about letting the bedroom set out of my sight for fear that it would get lost, but was assured by the wood finisher that Steven's furniture would not only be safe in his hands, but the work would be completed by the time we moved into our new house in December. I let the wood finisher pick it up from the rental house, but felt a nagging uneasiness about the set being out of my hands. I even called the gentleman a few times over the months to make sure that Steven's precious bedroom set was "doing okay." He probably thought I was a little crazy, but I really didn't care. I had given him an extremely important possession of ours, and felt he owed it his utmost care. About two weeks before we moved in, I called the wood refinisher to set up a date for delivery to coincide with our move, and was told that he never even got to the job due to an enormous custom cabinet order which consumed most of his fall season. I was mad at him, and more mad at myself for letting the bedroom set be gone for what I now considered no good reason. I had that familiar anxiety attack feeling come over me, and knew that I just needed to get the bedroom set back in my hands, bleached oak, scratches and all, and that maybe Steven's markings were meant to stay on the beloved and worn pieces.

When the men returned the set, it was the day after our move into the new house, and we were all exhausted. I not only felt as though the move, any move, wasn't right without bringing Steven with us, but all of our things needed to be unpacked and a new home needed to be created. Was I really up for this next challenge? Besides that fact, it was exactly one week before Christmas of 2004. There's probably no one in the world who wouldn't agree that a move is stressful any time of year, but the holidays make it especially awful, even under the most normal of circumstances.

So, piece by piece, the furniture got brought back in to us, up to the room which would soon become a guest bedroom in our new home. No longer Steven's room, no longer a living, breathing part of our home. Just a room for guests, should we have ever have a guest again or go back to any of the entertaining that we used to do. As the truck emptied, a new sense of panic emerged as I didn't see Steven's mirror come in, the rectangular oak mirror, which fastened on to his dresser. The truck stood empty, the wood refinisher not even remembering having Steven's mirror in his possession. I cried and cried at the thought of how unnecessary it was to have even given up his furniture to anyone's care in the first place, now to have part of it lost. I needed all of Steven's things to join us at the new house; again, I needed Steven. I moved in slow motion for the next several hours, racking my brain to think of what could have become of the mirror. All of our moving boxes had been placed in the appropriate rooms, all accounted for and labeled. I visited the bedroom with Steven's furniture over and over again, looking at the place where the mirror should have been, feeling sick and furious with myself for having let it out of my sight.

The next day, our carpenter arrived to assemble and affix a Pottery Barn locker cabinet to the wall of our mudroom. The boxes to the locker set had been blocking the entrance to our garage, and we were eager to put it up. They were all stacked against one wall, all labeled "Fragile," and all had the Pottery Barn logo on them. The carpenter opened all of the bigger crates carefully, and finally came to a last box, an unmarked one, which hid beneath all the ones labeled "Pottery Barn." As I stood watching him, I know now that there was a reason why that box was last. The brown cardboard rectangle, professionally wrapped and filled with packing papers, held the most important moving item for me. Of course, it was Steven's bedroom mirror. A sign for all of us, but especially for me that indeed, my little boy came with us to the new house, and that his mirror never made it to the wood refinisher after all.

Mother's Day will always, always be difficult for any mom who's lost a child. The once happy holiday now only causes unhappiness, and has greatly bothered me since that very first one. Much like Father's Day for my husband, you wish you could bypass the day and simple move onto the other 364 days of the year when being a mother or father isn't "celebrated." Even though we're blessed with still having two amazing daughters and have every reason to be proud of them every day of the year, these holidays force recognition to a role in life that's been stripped down to its bare bones of survival. Doesn't sound like party time, does it?

When each of my three children was in fourth grade, their school art project for Mother's Day was to make a cookbook with combined recipes from all of the kids in their homeroom. They would begin by trying to remember a favorite recipe from home and write it down from memory, including it on one page of the book. Then, they would secretly get the real recipe from home somehow and it would be on the opposite page. The moms would always get a kick out of receiving this special cookbook because the recipes that the kids wrote featured foods "baked at 100 degrees for twelve hours" or some like interpretation, but then they'd also get lots of accurate new recipes for their kitchens. It was always a popular Mother's Day gift, and my 4th grade cookbooks were a treasure to me.

One Mother's Day after Steven left us, I was browsing for a recipe out of one of my regular cookbooks when I came upon Steven's 4th grade one. I could barely look at it, feeling that wave of self-blame which still enveloped me on occasion. My old wound reopened, me blaming myself again, letting my little boy out of my sight only to get killed. I picked up his cookbook, brushing my hand over the cover, when the accompanying card he had made me fell out of it. I didn't remember seeing the card since the day he gave me the gift. In Steven's precise, fourth grade printing, he had thought of an adjective to describe me which coincided with every letter of the words, "Mother's Day." I burst into tears as I read them, the water of them filling me with Steven's life.

M-marvelous mom
O-on top of everything
T-the best
H-helpful
E-extraordinary

R-really nice
S-super mom
D-delightful
A-always caring
Y-you are the best mom in the world.

Then, he simply signed, "Love, Steven." Finding this homemade card at Mother's Day was exactly the sign I needed, and knew it was just for me.

One blustery fall day, I left my grief counseling session especially emotional. The sessions were getting really intense as I was digging into the deepest aspects of my grief process. I headed to my car in the midst of a strong wind, a chill in the air that gave me the impending feeling that winter wasn't far away. As I hurried to my car, something made me look to three large trashcans lined in a row near to where I parked. Suddenly, one of the cans, the middle one, tipped over. It so startled me that I felt goose bumps rush over me from head to toe. Other than the autumn wind, there was nothing and no one around to move this trashcan. It had to be a sign from Steven. He was my middle child, and I had just spent the last hour crying over the loss of my middle child. To me, it was a sign. To someone else, it might not be anything more than an isolated incident on a windy Chicago afternoon.

Although my life had been immersed in three's before Steven's accident, three kids, buying things in threes, etc, I had come to hate "two's." I didn't want "two," I wanted to go back to "three." Seeing things like the two Maples leaves was of great comfort to me as I labeled all future signs in "two's" as those from Steven, for him and me alone.

The summer of 2005, I began to have a recurring visit each day when I'd retrieve the mail from my mailbox. Two little finch birds would flit from my mailbox to the mailbox at the house next door. Back and forth, they'd chase each other, tiny yellow birds in a flutter of blurred wings, mailbox to mailbox. I would think of Steven and me when I saw the finches so many days that summer, two together, together forever.

I also always see two male cardinals together, always, always crossing my path, always crossing in front of me, my favorite color red, my favorite sign from Steven. Did the cardinals and the finches visit my world before Steven's death? They may very well have. I'll never know because I didn't notice them back then.

I have a photo of a little miraculous sign that Steven left for me the first Valentine's Day after we moved into the new house. It was early on a Sunday morning, close to Valentine's Day, and our daughter Brianna called me to the front window. It had snowed about an inch or so the night before, and a dusting of fluffy white snow remained on our driveway as no one had walked on it yet, not even for the Sunday paper, which lay on the parkway grass. The blanket of white looked like just that, an untouched fluff of blanket covering our driveway. Unbelievably, in the middle of the snow, without any footprint or movement around it, were two perfect hearts carved into the white. The hearts were almost intertwined, perfectly close to one another, two simply shaped messages for a Valentine's Day from heaven. The hearts lying within an untouched covering of snow were surely from Steven, a phenomenon unexplainable to anything else. Although the hearts could have been for any of us, I took them as a sign to me, only because I had been thinking of Steven so much that weekend. I had been thinking about the Valentine's Day of 2003 two short years prior, when I gave each of the three kids a subscription to their favorite magazine, and gave Steven "Sports Illustrated for Kids." He loved it, and I've kept the subscription going even since his journey to heaven. We still give each issue to a little boy or girl we know who would appreciate this magazine. Steven's "Sports Illustrated" issues have gone to our own kids, our nieces and nephews, friends of Steven's, anyone in our lives who enjoys reading about the lives of today's sports heroes, and who would enjoy a little gift from Steven. Also, in a comforting way, it has helped us to have little bits of Steven's life that didn't have to end, one of them being the subscription to his favorite magazine. So that Valentine's Day weekend, I received a special gift from my little boy. Inside of the untouched snow, two hearts said, "Happy Valentine's Day from your boy."

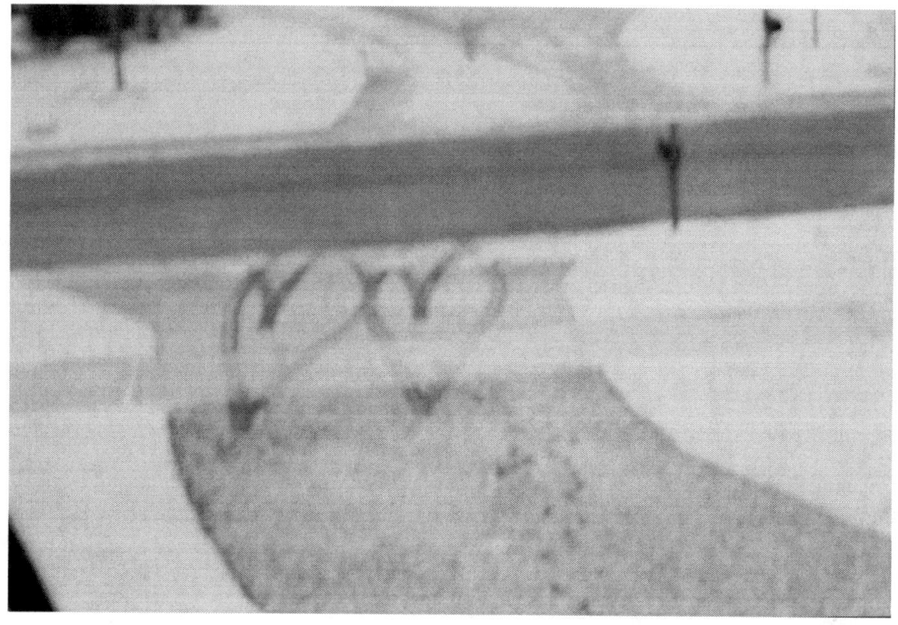

I didn't have the need for signs representing Steven and I before April 19, 2003. I was too busy living life and taking it for granted like everyone else. I didn't need to attach any symbolism to birds or leaves or snow hearts, or much of anything for that matter. Now, I view the signs as my son's continued deep connection with me. And it's okay that some of the signs are for his mom alone. As I said, I especially need those.

* * *

CHAPTER 18: IF YOU BUILD IT, THEY WILL COME

Some of the signs from Steven were put into motion in the first days after his death, but not brought to fruition until much later. Like the baseball field we dedicated in his name.

We knew of parents who lost a child and set up scholarship funds, who donated to the research of the illness that took their child's life, giving back in the hopes of helping another child in need or preventing another tragic loss. We, of course, were committed to uncovering the details of Steven's accident, to finding out what exactly happened in those brief seconds at the train crossing. We also knew we would do what we could to help make railroad crossings safer for pedestrians in general, and to make children more aware of train danger and how quickly something fatal can happen. Still, these were longer term goals that would be handled in private, and had nothing to do with the task at hand, that being what we would do with the donations we would receive in Steven's memory.

With our decision at the funeral home that Easter morning, Lake Forest Parks and Recreation was named in the obituary as the recipient of any monetary gifts. In discussing the idea further, we estimated that, with these donations, we'd be able to provide a new game table of some sort for the kids to enjoy in the game room and thought that this small token in Steven's memory would be appreciated by the kids who frequented the park district facilities after school hours and on weekends.

Before we knew it, the donations starting coming in, many more and in larger numbers than anyone had anticipated, and soon there were new decisions to make.

We always knew we were blessed to live in a very generous, thoughtful community. We just never realized how generous until the dollars started accumulating. Along with many wonderful donations from family and close friends, Steven's park district fund was quickly numbering into the tens of thousands. We realized that we would not be limited to a small gift in Steven's memory, but something that could really make a difference in our community. The answer became clear. With my husband and son's love of baseball, the budget we were now looking at, and the in-kind donations of labor and materials we were suddenly being offered, we would gift a much-needed baseball field renovation in Steven's memory to the city of Lake Forest. *If you build it, they will come.* The line from the famous Kevin Costner movie kept replaying in our heads. The goal was lofty and the work ahead would not be easy, but the idea of building a new baseball field was something we knew we wanted to pursue. We would give hundreds of children who, like Steven, ate, slept and worshipped baseball a "field of dreams," and with our budget growing day by day from donations pouring in, it would surely be, in Steven's own words, "Sweeeet."

Our field of dreams took shape over the course of about ten months. We began having regular planning sessions with members of the Lake Forest Parks and Recreation board in July of 2003 to get initial approval on our plans. Although this was only three months after Steven's death, the immediacy of the efforts to get this project going gave us, and my husband in particular, purpose and direction. To create a legacy for your loved one, to run a marathon promising to help wipe out cancer, to donate your energy to furthering a cause for someone you loved and lost, all provide meaning to an otherwise senseless tragedy. Indeed, the baseball field project felt like Steven swooshing down to his dad to give him something really meaningful to do in his little buddy's honor. Our thought was to take the run-down baseball field, almost directly across the street from our old house in Lake Forest, and completely renovate it. We had many local friends who were in the contracting and supply business, and so we had resources for everything from concrete and asphalt, irrigation, fencing, even an electronic scoreboard.

My husband's college friend, Brian Davis, was in the sign business, and graciously offered to provide an electronic scoreboard at his company's cost, and subsequently, a group of friends from Elmhurst College, Steve's alma mater, joined forces to generously donate the scoreboard to Steven's new baseball field.

Things were moving at a fast pace as we finalized plans and scheduled the excavation to begin in early fall, 2003. Our hope was to have the field playable by summer, sod and all, and so we needed a good deal of prep and foundation work to take place before our long Chicago winter. We were blessed to have the support of contractors who donated their time and provided materials at their cost. Every area, from demolition and excavating by our dear friend, Carl, the same Carl who stayed by our side at the emergency room, to the creation of a paver brick memorial area in the shape of a baseball, by another dear friend and expert mason, George Galassini, would be constructed by people who personally knew Steven, who cared about us, and who had children of their own. Our "dream team," as we called it, was born.

The personal tribute we would pay to our son was a life-size bronze statue in the memorial area of the field, a replica of a treasured photo of Steven in his catcher's uniform, wearing his favorite number "13," holding a cast bronze baseball by his side which would be signed by the three of us, filled with messages of love and longing for the boy who would never play this earthly game again, but who would surely enjoy watching the games from above. We enlisted the talents of a gifted sculptor from the Northwest suburbs of Chicago. His name was Joseph Burlini, and by the end of his journey of creating a "Steven" statue for the park, we felt like Joe knew Steven himself. Joe even let me work on Steven's face when it was still in clay, and touching the soft, warm putty of what would be Steven's cheeks, nose, forehead, did much to allay my fears of the cold rigor mortis, which had for so long overshadowed the last time I touched Steven's face. The pliable clay felt like soft skin, and nothing like my experience from the wake and funeral.

My husband spent long hours at the field, physically helping where he could, simply going for "lunch runs" for the many people who dedicated countless hours of their personal time to make this project happen. My husband's Italian beef sandwiches and fries from our local burger joint fed many a hungry volunteer all those months, and their dedication to our project "fed" us, spiritually and emotionally.

Even our donations took on new life when word of the new baseball field got out. New donations came in from folks in the community who wanted to support a city improvement that would benefit so many kids. They came from our local baseball organizations wanting to formally express their gratitude for our efforts to better their programs. Everyone "stepped up to the plate," so to speak, and we are forever grateful to everyone who made May 23, 2004 a day that we not only gave birth to a new state-of-the-art playing field at Everett Park in Lake Forest, IL, complete with dugouts, a home run fence, warning track, and that unbelievable scoreboard, but a day in which we committed to new baseball memories in Steven's name, where little guys would play the game that Steven loved so dearly and never said "no" to a chance to play. I was overwhelmed at the magnitude that the project took on, but humbled every step of the way by the love and support of those who helped make it happen.

The dedication was full of symbolism, as an arc of balloons in the colors and shape of a rainbow graced the home plate area, spring flowers bloomed around the baseball-shaped memorial area, and a path of inscribed paver bricks led the way to the statue of Steven, our beloved little catcher. Everyone and anyone who made a donation to the field project received a brick, regardless of the dollar amount of the donation. There were no "friends of Steven," or "very special friends of Steven" tiers of donors; all were treated the same and given any random spot on the walkway, from the larger corporate sponsors, to the small scout troop who made a donation to Steven's field of dreams, to the classmate who donated her babysitting money. At the base of the bronze statue, a home plate shaped dedication plaque was inscribed with the words,

This baseball field is hereby dedicated
May 23, 2004
to our son and brother,
Steven Brian Malin, Jr.
Born
January 20, 1992
"Drafted" by God
April 19, 2003
A boy who lived and loved life to its fullest,
who never gave up no matter what the score,
and whose smile, spirit and sportsmanship
will shine down on the players
who enjoy this field
for many years to come.

All our love forever,
Mom, Dad, Francesca, Brianna and "Scooby"

The ceremony itself began with the first raising of the flag by our local American Legion Post 264, then a tribute by the choir of our church. Our pastor, Fr. Bill McNulty, would lead a blessing of the field, all of our hands in an outreached gesture bringing God to the forefront of our efforts. Two of our many nephews, Jordan Malin and Michael DiVito, in their own baseball uniforms, would lead the Pledge of Allegiance. All of the Lake Forest house and travel league boys would proudly wear their uniforms. Our own daughters would release the rainbow of balloons that officially opened the field. We would announce, one by one, our "dream team," who worked so tirelessly over that year to create the beautiful field we now stood upon. A "dream team" plaque, directly across from Steven's statue, would read in part:

With deepest gratitude,
The Malin family acknowledges
and thanks the following members
of our "Dream Team," whose
time, talent and tireless effort
made this baseball field a reality.

The plaque went on to name each person, contractor and vendor who had so generously contributed to making the field a reality. Words from the director of our Parks and Recreation department, Mr. Fred Jackson, would express the feelings of our community, a town grateful for this amazing place to play ball. Finally, Steve and I would speak, thanking each and every person who played a part in the project, reminiscing once again about Steven, sharing the sentiments of our family just one year later. It was a wonderful event, capped off by hot dogs and baseball fare. We felt good about the day, and although it threatened rain, the weather held out for us. We grabbed a quick bite for dinner afterward, and missed a surprise finale that appeared over the sky some minutes after we cleaned up and left the field. What else but a rainbow colored the sky that dusk. We knew Steven would have loved to have had it appear about twenty minutes earlier, but I guess when you're a young angel, you still have to perfect your special effects.

210
205

Our dog, Scooby, sits by a tree donated to the field by the Kariotis family.

Creating the baseball field created a purpose beyond playing a game there. It represents a quiet place of reflection for us, but, more importantly, a place for life and the living where there are no tombstones or crypts, only dugouts and home run markers, a place where we, too, can feel alive, and feel Steven's life. Steven only played at Everett Park in its original state, and although he will never play there again, we are comforted by the fact that so many children will enjoy this special place for years to come.

Like so many nights before, sleep eluded me the night of the dedication. I tossed and turned, thinking of yet another turn of events, another opportunity for the word "bittersweet" to enter my vocabulary, bitter grief and sweet memories. And again, Steven visited my dreams.

I was at the baseball field, watching the young children run the bases, their hair flying in the wind, wearing smiles from ear to ear. Suddenly, among the boys, Steven ran by me. He turned each of the bases like a child of boundless energy, his happiness in running the infield as evident as the expression on his face. I called out to him, realizing that he was not the eleven year-old that I remembered. He was younger, more juvenile, maybe around age the age of eight.

As I continued to watch him run the bases, I had a sudden worry overtake me as I remembered that Steven would not have the opportunity to live his full life, and it equated to the fact that he had limited "oxygen," and the "oxygen" would run out at age eleven.

I began shouting to Steven to stop running, but he wouldn't listen to my pleas. I needed him to stop, to conserve his oxygen, to not have it run out too soon as I knew he was only given a limited supply. He only kept smiling, his face red with exhilaration, his fun in running the bases taking precedence over me begging for him to stop and save what oxygen he had left. I cried and screamed to him, but nothing would stop Steven from enjoying every minute of his day at the baseball field.

I awoke in a familiar cold sweat, and sat upright for a long time, trying once again to make sense of another visitation. This time, I had the benefit of my work with Alan to derive meaning from the symbolism in the dream. As I sat in bed that night, I remembered something I said as I eulogized Steven at his funeral. "*They say it is better to have ten minutes of 'Wow' than a lifetime of 'Blah.' Well, Steven, you gave us eleven and a quarter years of the finale on the Fourth of July.*" And so I realized that, if Steven had a choice of running the bases or sitting on the sidelines conserving his energy so he'd have more time on this earth, he'd choose to run the bases. This was the little boy we called our son. He was true to himself to the last breath he took. He "ran the bases" of his life with the gusto that some people never live to experience in eighty years of living. I guess I should've been happy that, in my dream, Steven wouldn't sit down. He ran and ran, and celebrated the joy that every moment of his life and his day at the field of dreams had to offer.

Suddenly, the dream was a joyous affirmation that my little boy lived a life that I should live, that we all should live. When I visit the baseball field at Everett Park, I think of the dream that night, and I envision Steven running the bases, red-faced and full of life, life the way he chose to live it. *Thank you, Steven, for giving our lives such "life."*

* * *

CHAPTER 19: RAINBOWS FOLLOW HAIL

> *And God said, "This is the guarantee of the covenant I am making with you and every living creature with you, a covenant for all subsequent generations: I will place my rainbow in the clouds, and it will become a guarantee of the covenant between me and the earth: Whenever I bring clouds over the earth and the rainbow appears in the clouds, then I will remember my covenant with you and with all living creatures of all kinds. Never again will the waters become a flood and destroy all living things. When the rainbow is in the clouds, I will notice it and remember the perpetual covenant between God and all living creatures of all kinds that are on the earth."*
>
> *Genesis 9:12-16*

Indeed, rainbows have colored our lives since that magical day at the school baseball field. Rainbows became an extremely important sign for our family and even for our community, especially for the many who witnessed the first rainbow at the baseball tournament with us. Rainbows are the promise that God keeps His covenant, and to us, this means Steven's eternal life. Rainbows are the promise that God has not abandoned us, not forgotten us, not left us alone to forever face the storms and sadness. *The Lord God said, "I will not forget you. See? I have engraved you on the palms of my hands."* The rainbows have come to us at the most meaningful of times, there to provide evidence of Steven's presence with us, as well as the promise that God has Steven safely with Him. I don't remember there being so many rainbow sightings before Steven's journey to heaven. I remember a photo I had taken of Francesca's first rainbow sighting when she was around five years old, her innocent face looking out the window at the beautifully painted arc outside. After that, I barely saw rainbows. I remember us driving to a graduation party in 2002 and our family seeing a rare double rainbow out the car window, us being speechless at the sight, none of us remembering the last time we'd seen a single rainbow let alone a double. Yet rainbows have appeared fairly often since that first rainless rainbow in 2003 at the memorial tournament. The rainbows come dramatically, unexpectedly, and always at times when we most need a sign.

One day that first winter after Steven's death, I was driving home from an afternoon grief counseling session with Alan. I was trying hard to keep control, driving and at the same time replaying in my mind the draining work at Alan's. On this cold and dreary Chicago afternoon, I decided to stop over at my parents' house and visit for a little while to break my thought process away from the therapy session. Many times when I'd leave Alan's office, I'd be completely exhausted from crying and working through the new challenges of life post-Steven. I would have to clear my head, and running a few simple errands afterward, doing anything close to "normal" helped alleviate those heavy feelings.

About four blocks from my parents' home, a wet, freezing snow began hitting my windshield. My mind had been racing the entire car ride from the visions re-created during the grief counseling session, and the snow only served to reinforce the cold, nightmarish feelings I had just relived. Out of nowhere and entirely out of line with our winter weather, the snow turned to hail. To no avail, cars tried to quickly put on their windshield wipers as the snow-hail was blinding. The hail reminded me of the incident in my car the day prior to the coroner's inquest, and I could barely keep my hands on the steering wheel. I was about a block from a dear old friend's house, a loving young woman named Alexa Karkazis, and quickly pulled off the road toward her street. I called her from my cell phone and luckily found her at home. In my hysterical voice, I asked if I could pull into her garage, knowing that she had an extra parking space, until the hail subsided. She opened her garage door for my car and her home to me for my obvious shaking and distress. A glowing fire was lit in her cozy family room, and she welcomed me in to calm down and warm up. After a cup of tea and some soothing words, I began to feel better. The hail had only lasted a few more moments after I arrived at her door. Still, we sat and visited for a long while, and I never left to finish the drive to my parents' house. Alexa had gone through the loss of her own beautiful infant daughter, Eleni, years before, and was just the right person at that moment to know what to say and what not to say to me. I stayed for almost an hour, although the comfort I received there made it feel like a lifetime. As I got ready to leave, the sun had come out, probably to confirm that this was indeed a most unusual winter day in Chicago, also to tell me that it was okay to get back in my car. A few moments before I left, Alexa pointed out her patio window, and in the midst of this discombobulated winter day, which now saw snow, sun and hail, I witnessed a glistening, perfectly-hued rainbow. I stood riveted with her, absorbing the symbolism, the counseling session, the weather. But of all the emotion I felt inside, I mostly felt gratitude. Gratitude for the presence of Alexa when I needed an "Alexa" to welcome me in from the hail. Gratitude for the rainbow when I so needed the beauty of it to bring Steven to me, when I needed a "Steven" sign to bring closure to this dramatic day. Definitely a day when my blessings added up quickly.

As we sat in church on the morning of Steven's first anniversary in heaven, April 19, 2004, my husband and I had a few voice mails waiting on our cell phones. The messages told of a rainbow that appeared to a few of our friends who were driving to downtown Chicago that morning. Our friends wanted to share the experience, knowing how much comfort it would bring to us in the midst of this difficult day.

One night at the beginning of the summer of 2005, we were on our way to dinner at The Lake Forest Club, a small bath and tennis club we belong to near our home. Tradition held that many families from our town all had dinner there the Friday night of Memorial Day weekend, the official opening of the season there, parents socializing, the kids going for a night swim after dinner, weather permitting. We had mixed emotions about going to the club that evening, not only due to the familiar longing for our son to be with us, but also because the manager of our club and friend, Steve Parisi, had died suddenly over the winter, and we knew that the summer season wouldn't be the same without him there.

As we pulled out of our driveway and toward the club, we were greeted by a much-needed sign. There, ahead of us on the short drive over, was a double rainbow. Was it Steven and our dear friend reassuring us to go that evening? Were they there together in heaven giving us a sign that all was good with them? We sure thought so. And so did Steve's wife, Mary Kay, who also worked at the club and shared a big hug with us that night about the very same double rainbow.

My very close childhood friend, Maria Kariotis, called me about a symbolic double rainbow she witnessed one day after the loss of a child in her community. In 2004, a young boy around Steven's age that lived near her home, Victor, was also hit and killed by a train. This tragedy had obviously greatly impacted her community, and Maria often spoke to me about Victor's mother and how his family was coping. As Maria sat stopped at that fateful train crossing one rainy day the next year, she daydreamed of Steven and this other boy, and thought of how special it would be if they knew each other in heaven, playing baseball together as they both loved to do. Out of nowhere, a double rainbow appeared over the train tracks in front of her. She immediately called me, emotionally filled with the depth of this most profound sign at this most improbable moment. We reflected on it and cried over the phone together, and the thoughts I now have of this wonderful boy and his family, bring me to that day and the double rainbow when Maria received the message of God's promise.

Steven would have graduated 8th grade from Deer Path Middle School in June of 2006. Steven was remembered in a special section of the graduation video as many of his classmates had thoughtfully submitted photos of themselves with Steven to be included in the video montage. His class also held their last field trip and last annual baseball tournament at Steven's baseball field at Everett Park. The day was a joyous one, complete with exciting competition, music from student disk jockeys, lunch, and a small memento from our family. I wrote a short poem from Steven and had it printed onto a rainbow-embossed bookmark for each of the graduates. The poem read,

> *I am watching over you, although you cannot see me.*
> *I am walking by your side, although our shoulders no longer touch.*
> *I am cheering on your home run from a farther place across the field.*
> *I am guarding your path, praying that each step you take*
> *brings you closer to your goals and dreams.*
> *If you're ever in doubt, just look up.*
> *I'll be the sun warming your day,*
> *the wind pushing you along, the rainbow coloring your sky.*
> *I am forever your friend.*
> *I know that we'll be together again,*
> *but until then, I'll be watching over you.*

No matter the love and support we felt at all the gestures from Steven's class at graduation time, the deep sorrow we felt at his missing this most important milestone was so heavy to carry. The 8th grade parents gathered at a home the evening of the graduation dance and were kind enough to include us, but we knew that we would be anything but good company on this night, and didn't want to bring them down with our somber mood.

At the time that the kids were all being dropped off for the dance at school, our phone began ringing. We hesitantly answered it only to find out that a rainbow had appeared, seemingly hanging over the middle school, its brightly colored hues decorating the arrival of Steven's classmates for their most important night of celebration. Parents were calling us to make sure we saw it, their kids so excited at this timely "hello" from Steven who they were certain was wishing them a fun evening. We all sat quietly on our front porch, Steve, the girls and I, silently crying and absorbing the sight of the rainbow which did, indeed, look like it purposely hung over the school. *Dear God and Steven, thank you for showing us the promise of your covenant this evening. Thank you for letting us know you are near and that Steven's friends know he is present on their most important night.*

Our younger daughter, Brianna, whose birthday is in June, wanted to have her 12th birthday party at the Lake Michigan beach near our home. Unfortunately, the weather was completely uncooperative to host this outdoor "beachfest" featuring a DJ, pizza and dancing, as the night's forecast promised and delivered a cool, drizzly evening for the kids. We made the best of it, lighting a huge bonfire in the beach pavilion and kept the party guests under the protective cover of the alcove where they were still able to enjoy being outdoors but protected from the rhythmic patter of the rain.

As the evening went on, the rain eventually stopped, and the skies over the lake actually began looking like we'd have the last of a beautiful sunset. We had been teasing Brianna the whole week prior to the party that if her big brother had his way, there'd never be boys at her birthday or within a ten-mile radius of her and her sister, for that matter. I guess we were teasing her in vain. What, over Lake Michigan appeared at the party than a beautiful arc of a rainbow, there to send our daughter and Steven's little sister a big Happy Birthday wish. The kids, most of whom knew of the meaning of rainbows to our family, rushed out to the giant stone half-wall near the water's edge to pose for a photo in front of the rainbow, all waving and pointing to the big message for Brianna, their smiling faces a vivid remembrance of a rainbow that brought magic to this birthday celebration.

Brianna has been fortunate enough to have a rainbow appear on her 14th birthday as well, at the occasion of my dear friend Maria's daughter Alexandra's 8th grade graduation party. Of course, it was a double celebration and so warranted a double rainbow. We know that if Frankie's birthday wasn't in November, she'd have rainbows from her little brother, too.

So yes, rainbows are a most definite sign to us of the promise of eternal life, of the promise that God keeps His covenant with us, that Steven is there to send a "hello" to all who he doesn't want to say good-bye to, either. We are all bound by our human existence in this life, but are connected to each other by the belief in the immortal signs from above, again, if we choose to see them. For us, the rainbows not only provide color to our lives, but further ingrain in us the evidence of Steven's continued connection to us. And although I still sometimes fear hail, I always look for rainbows.

* * *

CHAPTER 20: MORE STEVEN SYMBOLS

Our son loved the number "13," and chose it whenever he could on his sports jerseys for football, basketball or baseball. My husband always wore 13 on his jersey as well, and I think that Steven found it cool that his dad would always pick the "unlucky" number on purpose, defying luck and counting instead on talent and effort to bring his success in sports. Steven followed his dad's love of the number 13, and the fun of wearing the least lucky number. My husband had played a season in the minor leagues just out of college, a pitcher for the San Francisco Giants organization, and wasn't allowed to wear 13. So, he proudly wore number "31."

After Steven left us, we'd get calls here and there from family members who now wanted to wear "lucky 13." Our brother-in-law Randy, Steve's brother who is full of life with three boys of his own, would call and tell us of one of the boys unexpectedly getting number 13 assigned to them for their football jersey. Brianna once found herself with soccer jersey number 13 after her coach made a last-minute switch due to sizes.

Being in the middle of the alphabet with our last name beginning with "M," our kids have found themselves with the number 13 in a line-up or class list several times. Of course, this is nothing new as we've always been in the middle of the alphabet, but we now look for number 13's as signs from Steven. Brianna considers being assigned the number 13 as good luck, and was thrilled to get it for a Poms tryout in 8th grade. She even kept her tryout sheet with the safety pin still attached as a remembrance of her big brother watching over her that day during her important tryout.

We have had family members call us up to say that they were at the deli counter of the grocery store and were given ticket number 13 or that they were at a movie and their movie ticket ended in 13, and these occurrences brought Steven into their day. Getting number 13's could have happened a hundred times before, but was never looked upon as any symbol of anything. In fact, getting a number 13 prior to April of 2003 for these folks may have been purely "unlucky."

We now realize that row 13 is frequently available on airplanes. We grab it whenever we can because we know that although others may feel it is unlucky, it makes us feel that Steven is closer to us on the flight.

We have nephews who have the number 13 in their screen names, and buddies of Steven's and family friends who consider the number 13 their "lucky" number now. They not only want it on their jerseys, but even their AOL accounts. The number is lucky to all of us because it's a symbol of Steven. It's him popping into our day, our sports event, our email, our jersey assignment, our tryout, even our visit to the deli counter.

During Steven's years in a local football and basketball league called "New Vision Athletics" or NVA, he always begged his coaches to have the number 13 assigned to him for "good luck." The program was run by a wonderfully mentoring coach and dad named Kraig Moreland, and Kraig's methodology of teaching the kids proper skills development and good sportsmanship above the competition aspect made it a truly unique and worthwhile program for these young kids.

Kraig contacted us during the fall of 2003 with an idea. He wanted to end the NVA fall sports award banquet that season with a dedication to Steven. He wanted to retire Steven's number 13. He had compiled a montage of Steven playing in the various years he participated in the football and basketball programs with NVA, and wanted to play the video that night and remember Steven with the retiring of his favorite number. This was not a reflection of Steven's superstar status in either of these sports; Steven was neither tall enough nor beefy enough to be stellar in basketball or football. Nevertheless, we were honored that Kraig was motivated to this wonderful gesture simply because he considered Steven a role model of good sportsmanship.

As I sat at the awards banquet, I looked around, once again trying to grasp onto the meaning of what was happening as well as trying my best to keep my emotions in check. I saw the familiar faces of Steven's past teammates waiting patiently for their names to be called for their usual end-of-season awards, goofing off with their buddies here and there in between. Again, I wondered about our fate that Steven would be the recipient of the memorial that night instead of simply being there waiting to be called up with his team. How did it come to be that we were lucky enough to have a child who was honored for good sportsmanship, yet unlucky enough to not have him there to receive the honor?

Out of nowhere, I thought of a sheet of paper we kept hanging on our bulletin board in the back hallway of our home. I had come across it some weeks before. It had been hanging in the back hall since 2001, so Steven himself knew the tattered piece of green paper well. It was a quote by John Luther, and reads, "*Good character is more to be praised than outstanding talent. Most talents are, to some extent, a gift. Good character, by contrast, is not given to us. We have to build it, piece by piece — by thought, choice, courage and determination.*"

I couldn't control the fate that our Steven was gone and wouldn't be there himself to hear that this wonderful coach who thought he exhibited good sportsmanship. I could, however, still be proud of Steven and feel gratitude for this extraordinarily thoughtful gesture. Being rewarded for being a good person is like winning the Olympic Gold for what really matters in life — how you treat others. And I guess others thought he was really good at that. He was called a "gentleman" on and off the field, happy for his teammates' success, remembered for cheering on his team whether they were winning or losing. *Steven, I'm so proud of you. Are you hearing all these kind words in your honor?*

The award night that November evening ended up meaning so very much to our family, and Steven's best buddies Bobby and Garrett were even speakers at the event. Again, they were asked more than their age or innocence should have asked of them, but we witnessed young boys who rose to the occasion, who were eloquent and mature, and whose presence there were the ultimate "presents" to us.

On our last day of spring break in Marco Island, Florida, the five of us had gone on a wave runner tour to go dolphin watching. Steven loved dolphins, and counted, what a surprise, "thirteen" dolphins that day. We'll never really know if there were thirteen, but laughed that Steven made sure the dolphins totaled his favorite number in the world. Beautiful, majestic, jumping dolphins. It was a special way to end a wonderful spring break vacation, and we talked of dolphins all through dinner that night. Steven had a true fascination with the creatures, always sketching the same dolphin on his school folders, on our note pads at home, anywhere he would find a spot to draw a dolphin jumping through the water. He begged to swim with the dolphins, but our family vacations up until that point had not taken us to a "dolphin-swimming" locale, and Steven and Brianna hadn't been old enough yet, needing to be twelve to do so.

A few weeks after Steven's death, my husband and I went to watch Brianna's first softball game of the season, and it was cold and miserable outside. I had added many layers to my clothing, and still froze watching the game. My brother, Gene, had stopped over that evening for a visit after the softball game and was waiting in our driveway when we got home. We sat comfortably in our family room, the fireplace warming up our chilled bones, the kids around us. Brianna sat between my brother and me on the couch, quietly doing her homework, when conversation naturally shifted to a topic of Steven. We talked for a long while, and unbeknownst to me, Brianna had long finished her assignments and had gone on to drawing. Although Brianna had many gifts, her eight year-old art usually consisted of stick figures and flowers, and had not as yet developed into her ability today (better stick figures and flowers...just joking, Bri). Yet that night, she sat peacefully drawing, and when she was done, showed me her work. It was a beautiful dolphin. But actually, it wasn't Brianna's dolphin; it was Steven's. The dolphin he had drawn so many times, and that Brianna had never drawn until that night stood proudly on her school paper. Her dolphin captured the lines and movement of Steven's dolphin to such a degree that it almost seemed as though his hand was guiding hers. In fact, that night we were all sure that it was. As the evening closed and we had all warmed up, I removed the sweatshirt and fleece I had been wearing all night. Under my outerwear was the original t-shirt I had on from that afternoon. There, on the front of my shirt, was an arc of dolphins majestically jumping through water. I hadn't even remembered putting the shirt on that morning. But indeed, there they were, Steven's dolphins on my simple shirt, and there it was, one beautiful dolphin sketched from Brianna's hand on her school paper. Although we didn't have thirteen dolphins that night, we were certain that Steven was with us to show us those few special ones.

* * *

Steve and Steven relax at Disney's Vero Beach Resort.

Steven and I finish climbing the Sleeping Bear Dunes in Michigan.

Steven, Bobby and Garrett at the Shedd Aquarium in Chicago, 2002.

Scottsdale, Arizona

Steven's 9th birthday party with his buddies.

Our kids with Grandma Jennie and Papa Gene on New Year's Eve, 1999.

Steven at his 2nd birthday party.

Our kids at the Lake Forest beach.

4 18 '99

2002 Lake Forest Baseball- Indians

Steven enjoys football and photo-ops with his friends.

Francesca and Steven, Christmas 1992.

Steven and Brianna, Halloween 1999.

* * *

PART III:
LIVING IN OUR NEW WORLD

CHAPTER 21: THINGS LOST AND FOUND

How do you begin to live in a new world, and what becomes of the physical reminders of the old world? How do you transition and decide what should become of these precious, tangible items? Do you pack them away? Leave them be? When we moved, many of those questions were answered. Out of necessity, we had to pack up Steven's things. Because our old house sold before it ever went on the market, we only had six weeks to pack, and we packed in haste. Hence, a few of Steven's things got misplaced. We knew they came with us to the rental and then the new house, but like the bedroom mirror, anything even temporarily missing sent me into a tailspin.

Indeed, when you lose something as extremely precious as a child, you cannot bear the thought of another loss. Not the loss of another child, not another loved one, not another physical "anything." Although I had made such strides in my counseling and seeking out the signs and symbols from Steven provided enormous comfort, I spent a good deal of time worrying about another loss. I found myself obsessing over the safety of my two daughters, the well being of my husband, the constant whereabouts of everyone I loved, the location of every physical possession of our son's. I couldn't stand an ounce more thought of separation.

The intangible signs we had been receiving were giving us little "gifts" from Steven, small treasures too priceless to describe in words. On the other hand, Steven's physical possessions became somewhat of icons to me. They were symbols of every milestone he reached in his eleven years. Before we moved, I'd go into Steven's bedroom and pay a sort of "homage" to everything there because to me, all the items represented a life lived to its eleven year-old fullest. Steven's belongings were not only important because they detailed his life loves, activities and accomplishments, but because at some point, Steven placed them in their location. He reflected on where his golf trophy should go, where his lucky seashell should be displayed. Although his things stood on bedroom bookshelves, on tops of dressers, in closets and in messy drawers his entire life, once Steven was gone, I needed to touch, smell and obsess about each and every one of them. If I couldn't find something of Steven's, I'd start crying. If I couldn't locate it immediately, it would ruin my entire day. When I packed our house up, I sometimes couldn't remember where I stored something. Goodness knows that my memory suffered through all the insomnia. If the item never ended up resurfacing, I'd grieve over it as another unbearable loss.

Those first weeks when our house was filled with friends and family, I'd go to Steven's room alone, worrying over his things. I knew he had placed his Christmas and birthday money from that year in a secret hiding place, but didn't know where it was and never thought I'd really need to know where it was as long as Steven did. Suddenly, this money would consume every ounce of my mind for hours on end. Why didn't I know of Steven's secret hiding place? Shouldn't I know? I knew I had to protect these precious few hundred dollars, put it in the bank for him, keep it safe from I-had-no-idea-who because there wasn't anyone in our lives who would take it. I couldn't find the money. I cried over it, grieved over it, felt like another failure for not knowing its whereabouts. It wasn't even the fact that it was money per se; it was that there was another item of my little boy's that was now irretrievably lost, and the loss was too much to bear.

There was an afternoon in that first year that I came home to the girls in a state of hysteria in the family room. They were engaged in a tug-of-war game that had gone terribly wrong. Brianna, nine years old at the time, had taken it upon herself to use some old baby blankets from our upstairs linen closet for her doll. One of the blankets was from Steven's infancy. A simple afternoon of a little girl playing with her doll in the family room had quickly turned into a funny game of pillow fighting and blanket pulling between sisters when mom wasn't home. The unfunny part was that one of the precious baby blankets,

Steven's, got accidentally torn in the festivities. I couldn't compose myself enough to take the mature stance that this was an accident, and accidents happen. Instead, I cried with the girls at this unintentional damage of their brother's baby memento. Inside, I felt out-of-control at the sight of the colorful woven blanket that shielded their infant brother, never to be the same. Again, it was all too much for me. Had the baby blanket gotten torn under normal circumstances, I would have probably still been upset, but also attributed a normal amount of perspective to the incident as well. Sadly, I had none of this perspective left when it came to Steven's physical possessions.

I even punished myself with regret for things I did or didn't do just before Steven died. It was as if I wished someone had just told me that these would be the last weeks or months with our beloved boy. I would have been perfect and in total control, right? Nobody warned me that this was "it," that he would soon be leaving us. That any last "this" or "that" should be cherished to the nth degree because it was truly the "last." We'd all like to say that we strive to live each day as though it's our last, but do we? Can we possibly? Should we ever have to live thinking this is the last year of our child's life?

One example of deep regret over Steven's last birthday was losing the roll of film from his party. I am one of those mothers who doesn't get around to developing the roll of film from birthday parties or vacations right away. I always envy the moms who enclose a photo from the party with their child's thank-you note. For me, that would happen two months later. I had changed rolls of film during Steven's indoor golf-themed party in January of 2003 and dropped the full roll into the bottom of a bag of gifts, a careless and rushed move in the chaos of the event. The dozen or so boys invited to the party that day were full of energy and mischief, posing for photos and laughing their way through eighteen holes of neon-lighted putt-putt golf. Although I didn't remember seeing the roll of film as I emptied the gift bag at home that night, we realized that it must have fallen out and tried searching for it around the house about a week later. I had even called the golf place to see if anyone had turned in an undeveloped roll of film, to no avail. At the time, we regretted the loss of the pictures, but other than that, would not understand the ramifications of Steven's last birthday party until he was no longer with us. I still think of that roll of film and how I frantically tried to find it after Steven's death, thinking that it would somehow materialize, somehow find its way back to us because life would be too cruel to let those last smiling photos of all of his friends go lost in the garbage. It's sad how the loss of one roll of pictures could create such pain, but the roll represented a last birthday celebrated, last smiles with beloved buddies, last glimpses of a silly celebration for a normal eleven year-old kid who loved golf and being with friends.

I came to enjoy the fact that Brianna, being two years behind Steven, was able to wear a little of her big brother's athletic clothing for a while after he was gone. We allowed her to rummage through a few of his sports athletic wear items when she had the need for cold weather under-armor for outdoor soccer, or basketball shorts for the junior travel leagues she played in. It made her feel closer to her brother and gave us comfort to see his things being used instead of sitting stagnant.

One Sunday in fifth grade, Brianna was in a travel basketball tournament for a high school feeder team she played on. The team wore our high school jersey and blue and gold colors representing the "Scouts" of Lake Forest High School where we live. Brianna had taken Steven's favorite hooded Scouts sweatshirt out of his closet and worn it to the tournament. The day was long and the kids' equipment and duffel bags were moved many times during the event. The sweatshirt never made it home from the tournament. I regretted allowing her to wear it, and although it was an accident, had a hard time getting over the loss of that precious sweatshirt, the stitched Scouts emblem proudly displayed, remembering how much Steven loved wearing it himself. I felt like I grieved the loss of that possession because it represented a time when my son was playing travel basketball himself, when he was young and full of sports and loved to wear hooded sweatshirts so much that we'd have to peel the sweaty things off of him, fighting to get them into the washing machine.

The losses were just more separation, more good-byes to physical things we couldn't bear to lose. We grieved each loss as if it were a loved one. The tangible, the solid, the possessions felt like they were slipping through our fingers, and no amount of signs from above comforted these specific and difficult feelings of loss.

Two years after Steven was killed, my husband and I planned to meet another couple for a casual dinner and movie. They were our great friends, Raphaela and Kirk, and though it was a rainy weekend, we thought it might be good to get out for a bit.

I didn't know what to wear because it had been raining all day and the ground was now full of puddles. I went into my closet and sifted through my shoeboxes, all stacked fairly neatly in my closet, almost all the shoes either brown or black for fall and winter, and white or beige for spring and summer. I didn't want to wear leather shoes for fear of getting them water-stained, and really wasn't terribly fussy for my choice that evening as I would only be wearing comfortable jeans and a turtleneck sweater to see these wonderful friends for dinner and a movie.

I remembered a pair of short rain boots, micro-fiber black ones with a small heel that weren't favorites but would suffice for a night of rainy weather like this. I hadn't worn them in years and almost forgot I'd had them. As I pulled the box off the shelf, I heard a shifting of something inside that didn't sound like the boots. I opened the box and literally slid down the wall to the carpeted floor of my closet, my hands shaking and my eyes in a state of shock. In the corner of the old shoebox was a small dark-green canvas wallet, a sports wallet that a little boy had asked for a few Christmases before. The secret hiding place. The Christmas and birthday money. Every last dollar there, safely tucked into a simple wallet in a secret hiding place that an eleven year-old would think of as "safe." Inside mom's shoebox. Along with the money, a Disney World pass, a filled-out ID card that came with the wallet, and even a picture of our dog. All of it found and safe, never to be spent, forever to be cherished. It was such an important finding that I was filled with joy just holding the wallet, turning it over and over, even smelling it. The joy of finding that wallet stayed with me for a long time, and still does today. Many things lost. But a definite sign from our little boy that sometimes things "get found" again.

* * *

CHAPTER 22: "HOW MANY KIDS?"

I didn't venture too far away from the safe shelter of my new small world for a long time. I felt secure in this microcosmic existence of my life, where everything remained within arm's reach. Socially, I only met good friends for coffee or lunch, and Steve and I would meet dear friends for a casual dinner now and then. I was satisfied that overall my family seemed to be doing better. The signs were helping. We were sharing them with one another more and more. It was really, really enough for that time. I didn't want or need to meet anyone new. I didn't want to be asked any painful questions, didn't want this safe status quo to be challenged in any way. Heck, I didn't want to watch the local news. I liked the quiet, the peace that came with a quiet house. I used to thrive on the hustle and bustle, the noise of our family. Now I thrived on silence, concentrated on my family, moved forward in tiny steps, and stayed close to home.

I hadn't resolved many issues with my faith, but I was praying about it. I continued my dialogue with God, and knew that was at least a step in the right direction. In the meantime, I never hesitated to ask Steven to help the girls, to help us move forward. And I didn't have to hear his answers; I just looked for his signs.

At the times I did venture into the "new," I felt uncomfortable. New people were a threat to me. I didn't even want to sit at the new year of a school volunteer committee because we'd invariably go around the table, introduce ourselves, say how many kids we had, what grades they were in. I wanted to hide under the table until my turn had passed.

I faced the question of how many children I had for the first time during the summer after Steven died. It had only been three months, and my husband and I were reluctantly attending the wedding of a friend of his from work.

I really didn't think we were ready for this larger environment yet, but we decided to try. We were innocently seated at a cozy table of eight with three other couples, none of whom I knew prior to that night. I did not anticipate the question from one of the other women at the table. Up until that moment, I guess I hadn't met anyone new since Steven died.

But, as moms do, the question came up of how many children I had. It's the way moms get to know each other. Looking around the table, I squirmed and glanced helplessly in the direction of my husband who was in the middle of conversation with the other men. Should I say that I have three children and hope she doesn't ask me to elaborate on their ages? Do I say that I have two children and feel like I'm lying to myself, and the rest of the world? After all, I will always have three children. One just happens to be in heaven now. Given the immediate answer needed in this situation and the fact that I was feeling a major anxiety attack looming over me, I answered "three" and excused myself to the bathroom without any explanation to my husband. My pace quickened; I couldn't get out of the banquet hall fast enough to escape this god-awful situation. My palms were drenched and I felt lightheaded as I made my way to the ladies' room. I exploded into tears, realizing another painful reality of my new life, that of a mother with three children who will from here forward be denied the third. No speaking of Steven's recent baseball tournament, no picking him up from practice, no asking him to clean up his room, no watching him sleep peacefully in the safe nest of our home, no telling a new acquaintance that I have an eleven year-old son who'll be entering sixth grade in the fall. I now faced the dilemma of how to answer the simple question of how many children I had. Did I really need to meet anyone new? Didn't I know enough people in my life? I had been doing just fine staying close to friends and family. I sat there on the couch, my head in my lap, just outside the ladies' room, women staring as they'd walk past. Boy, I knew I wasn't ready to be out like this.

My husband appeared not long after I sat down, obviously suspecting I was gone far too long for a quick visit to the bathroom. I told him the sorry tale of my encounter at the dinner table, and that I didn't want to walk back into the reception. He sat with me until I felt ready to get up, and we walked arm-in-arm back to the car, back to the safe anonymity of our home.

Although we stayed close to home and friends and family that summer, the situation of meeting a new group of moms came up again that fall. I had thought long and hard about failing that night at the summer wedding, and now anticipated such an encounter at an upcoming charity luncheon I would attend with my sister, Diane. The event, which benefited Children's Memorial Hospital in Chicago, was a worthy annual fundraiser I had attended for many years. Six months had now passed, and this time, I thought, I would be more prepared for the "social" aspect of this event. I knew that I would inevitably be introduced to a few new faces, and needed to resolve myself to that and be more ready for it. Just thinking it through beforehand empowered me. I felt more confident that I could calmly meet someone new, and even discuss a little of my personal life if the situation called for it. Sounds trite to someone who hasn't been through the loss of a child, but just the mere attending of a social function was difficult enough given the level of grief we were going through. Getting dressed, going to downtown Chicago, exposing myself to this large venue was, itself, a huge undertaking in my life at that time.

I sat quietly at the luncheon table that day, and actually enjoyed the simple pleasure of listening to conversation that had nothing to do with me, my life, or April 19th 2003. Suddenly, the woman to my left innocently asked if I had any children. I said yes, and left it at that. Unfortunately for me, she asked *how many* children I had. I decided to tell the truth and say that I had three, and again, leave it at that, even throwing the conversation ball back in her court. I cleverly asked her to tell me *all about her children,* thinking that people naturally love talking about themselves and their own family, and this would deflect any further prying into my family makeup. She talked for several minutes, reveling in her kids' schools and friends and accomplishments, and when I believed we had successfully exhausted the discussion of family, she turned the conversation back to me. "So, how old are your kids?"

I looked over at my sister. She looked sympathetic, but without an answer. She had not anticipated the question, either. "Well," I said honestly, "I have three children. A daughter whose fourteen, a daughter whose nine, and a son whose now in heaven." Her mouth dropped. She apologized, "Oh, gosh, I'm so sorry to hear that. I...I just don't know what to say." I apologized. "I'm sorry, but I need to excuse myself." Again, I quickly left the room and fled for the safety of the ladies' room. And again, I cried my eyes out. I really thought I was ready to do this. I thought I was ready to head out into my new world and maybe even meet someone *new.* Why did it have to come back to this?

My sister soon followed and calmed me down enough to say that the woman felt horrible for putting me on the spot and everyone wanted me to rejoin the group. Truth be told, I was the one who felt horrible. How was I going to get past this? I knew I couldn't go through life without meeting new people. I didn't blame these innocent folks for making small talk to a fellow lunch guest. How was I ever going to get through this, and when would the day come that life wasn't full of these hurdles?

After these encounters, I took a long time and discerned my options. I asked Steven for guidance on how to get through this next challenge in life. Would I disconnect my social life to avoid being asked questions that would constantly bring me to tears? This was crazy, and needed my conscious objectivity and much help from above to get me through it.

So, here's what has worked for me: good, bad or otherwise. I have come to the realization that I can choose who in my future will know about my son's death, and I am under no obligation to explain, expound, or otherwise clarify how large or small my family is, just as there are countless other facts about ourselves that we choose or choose not to share with others. I say this because I am the type of person who naturally feels the need to explain everything from where I got my shoes on sale, to why I was late, to other factoids of life that most people don't feel the same need to explain. Steven's death, however, is so beyond the stratosphere of shoe purchases that I know now that it is a private subject for the exclusive audiences of my immediate loved ones and those few in life who I will choose to share it with. But this does not include everyone I meet on the street. I finally realized that I'm not denying Steven; I'm simply keeping my private life "private."

Now, when I do choose to entrust someone new with this precious piece of information about my family, I do it very carefully. I do it only after our relationship has grown to a level that makes it feel right in revealing, not because I ever feel *obligated* to do so, or because I feel I'm not being truthful if I don't share about my son.

And honestly, there are still some rare occasions where I am somehow pressed into sharing my precious Steven with someone I have just met. But now, I can calmly and with control say that I have two daughters here with me, and one son in heaven with God. And I can finally say it just that way. If they then proceed to offer their condolences, I thank them. I don't break into hysterics, I don't offer any further explanation, and I can walk away from the meeting knowing that I successfully, and with total honesty of heart, met someone new. I have replaced the fear of these situations with simple gratitude for a new acquaintance. In fact, I try to include being thankful for meeting a new person in my daily blessings. Just as any relationship grows (or not), or reaches new level of confidences (or not), so the same rule goes now with my sharing the story of Steven. This outlook has returned me to a place of peace in the social aspect of my life. I can actually say, "Nice to meet you," and mean it.

* * *

CHAPTER 23: TRAVELING WITH STEVEN

Until we moved away from our old house, the sounds of the trains haunted us. During our daily activities, we heard the trains. In our sleep, we heard the trains. This especially bothered my husband. The sounds kept him up night after night. He was so, so bothered by the trains, and it constantly tortured his rest. It's not that we didn't hear trains before, but back then they were benign trains, not evil ones that killed our child.

Those close to us encouraged us to sneak away for a few days of peace and a badly needed dose of "change of scenery." We were ensconced in the familiarity of our home and community, but realized that we also were living in somewhat of a fishbowl. However, the thought of traveling without Steven was unthinkable. It seemed as though we should never again enjoy a family vacation without all five of us there. The thoughts left us really guilt-ridden. We had always provided our children the familiar ritual of an annual spring break vacation. How would that ever happen again? Going on a brief vacation was the last thought entering our minds, but in reality, was needed more than ever for our family. We needed to escape, but had no map.

A few days away, a little time alone away from many of the watchful eyes around us, even a chance to be "anonymous" in a remote locale sounded like a good plan. However, even taking the initial actions to organize a few days away with our two daughters made us feel like traitors. From the basic steps of making an airline reservation for a party of four as opposed to a party of five, choosing seat assignments on the plane for "two and two" as opposed to "two and three" or "five across," not requesting a rollaway bed for a third child, all added up to pain and guilt.

So, we talked it out as a family. We discussed how we would feel traveling without Steven. We brainstormed on how we could keep Steven "with us" as we took this big step of going away. We decided that, for the first time we went out of town, it might be better and more comforting to travel with a few of our family members, as the girls didn't love the idea of being "the two of them" while away. So, the first decision was made. The plan would be to join my sister, her husband, and two of their three children for a long weekend in Laguna Beach, California. We all loved Southern California, and hadn't been there in years. No traveling alone, no reservations for a family of four that we weren't ready to make. Even the fact that one of Diane's sons, Vincent, Jr., couldn't join us due to college commitments, softened the reality of them being a party of five and us now only being four. We felt good about the prospect of a few days away with them, with the sincere hope that a temporary change of scenery in beautiful Southern California would help us all. While there, we also had planned to take a one-day trip down to visit our old neighbors, Carl and Margaret Apfelbach, who had moved to Coto de Caza, California a few years before. More of the familiar, the comforting hugs, the break we needed.

Planning the weekend away was one thing, but packing us up was another. I had dismal feelings of packing our luggage without packing Steven's. How could I not be bringing his clothing, bathing suits and swim goggles with us? Again, this foreign feeling of not doing for my child, not automatically gathering his supply of pajama's, cargo shorts and t-shirts to come along in our bags left me with the millionth slap of reality in this scenario. The night before we were to leave, I wandered into Steven's bedroom, my mind wondering if I could really go through with the trip. I opened the door to his closet and was immediately struck with all things Steven. His favorite Abercrombie shirts, his dark green robe from a past Christmas hanging on the wall hook, assorted old stuffed animals crowding his upper shelf, a new golf shirt, tags still on, that now he would never wear, all stared a hole in my heart. I reached out to embrace Steven's clothing in his closet, almost falling into the rack that stood so lonely and untouched from the daily activity of a child grabbing clothes, swapping them out, and rushing through the day-to-day exchange of dressing for school, sports or whatever an eleven year-old day might bring. All of it, now staring at me, still and lifeless. I hugged the clothes hanging there, squeezing the hangers together till they were lopsided. I unconsciously grabbed a few of his favorite shirts, ones he had worn just before his death, and breathed in deeply. Before I lost my son, I never realized the smell that remained on clothing after one wore it, even after washing. Although Steven's clothes smelled fresh, they carried the little boy fragrance I loved and missed so much still in them. Smelling Steven's clothing was not new to me, but this night I was especially in need of being close to Steven's things, knowing that his "things" would be staying home during our long weekend away. As I stood there, silent and still myself, I thought of something. Maybe a little of Steven could come with us on this trip. I took two of his t-shirts, still on their hangers, held them close to me, and quietly shut his closet door. As I went back to packing my own bag, I gently placed Steven's shirts in with mine. I wondered for a moment what Steve and the girls would think, but knew in my heart of hearts that they wouldn't mind. I found a great deal of peace in the simple act of bringing Steven's shirts on this weekend trip with us. They would hang next to ours in the hotel closet. This brought me solace. I also took a photograph of the three kids, placing it carefully in my luggage, and displayed it on the nightstand of our hotel room. I knew I could look at their three smiling faces together, even though only two of our children were physically on the trip with us. All three were with me in spirit.

The girls decided that the first thing that they wanted to do the morning after we got to Laguna Beach was to buy Steven a souvenir, something from this locale that let him know that he was first on their minds. It was such a good and positive idea, and I think it lessened the guilt we all felt at being on a long weekend without him.

They bought him a key chain that said, "Laguna Beach," a perfect memento for a little boy who loved to hang lots of key chains on his school backpack. The girls so liked the idea of getting Steven a souvenir that they thought they'd now get him one from everywhere and anywhere we visited as a family in the future; a museum, a waterpark, a baseball game. We'd purchase a souvenir for Steven so that anywhere we went, he'd know he was in our thoughts. Over the years, the souvenirs have also served as the proof that we have survived this most horrible loss together, as a family unit, and still provided our other children with outings and the quality family time they still so deserved.

We kept our promise to visit our friends from Lake Forest on our last day in Laguna Beach, and ventured down to their home and then on to the San Diego Sea World for the day. We had been to that Sea World about five years prior with our three kids, and had wonderful memories of getting splashed at the dolphin show there. The day was bittersweet, but it was good to see our friends from home and revisit a place we all loved. And of course, we bought Steven a souvenir. As we dropped the Apfelbach family back off to their Coto de Caza home that evening, we found a "visitor" on their driveway who we considered a little "hello" from Steven. A sign.

You see, these neighbors used to live across our back yard, and a small retention pond separated our yard from theirs. As we'd sit in one of either of our yards during summer evenings, we'd be serenaded by pond bullfrogs. So, what did we find on Carl and Margaret's driveway as we headed to our car? Naturally, a big old frog, there to make us laugh and remind us of the nights when bullfrogs shared our summer evenings. It also gave us a sign of Steven being close to us that day. We tried to find a "frog" souvenir the next day, with no luck, to remind us of the sign from Steven and the memory of the special day with our old neighbors. *Stevie, only you would think of the frog!*

As the first souvenirs accumulated that first year, maybe a handful or more from our family outings, we needed a place to put them. Again, as a family, we decided to make a memory box for Steven, a special place to put these little gifts for him. On Steven's birthday, January 20th, we set his place at the dinner table for this one special time, made one of his favorite dinners, and afterward, created the memory box as a family.

We collected old magazines, including Steven's Sports Illustrated for Kids issues that had been gathering since we had not cancelled his subscription, and along with glue, tape, scissors and a mid-size white Rubbermaid container, set out on our mission at the kitchen table to make Steven the best memory box in the world.

While we knew that the box would be decorated with lots of sports clippings, we also wanted to reflect other aspects of Steven's life and loves in the magazine snippets and photos that would adorn it. We found photos of Steven's favorite foods and treats, including steak and potatoes, Perdue chicken nuggets, dill pickles, Burger King onion rings, Oreo cookies and "slurpees" from 7-Eleven. We pasted on photos of Steven's sports heroes, including Ivan "Pudge" Rodriguez, Wayne Gretzke, Tiger Woods, Barry Bonds, Tony Hawk and Shaquille O'Neal. There were pictures of monkeys and puppies and a water park that Steven loved. Even a silly photo of actor Jim Carrey, Steven's favorite actor from the Ace Ventura movies, made its way onto his special box. We clipped and glued and placed all the pictures into a collage of everything Steven.

Making the memory box for Steven on his birthday not only gave our family something productive to do, but something to do for *him*. Going to a mausoleum, attending Mass or placing flowers at a gravesite are usual rituals at the times of the year when we acknowledge a "birth day" or "anniversary of death," but still being able to "do" for your lost loved one, to create a new something in their honor, like a memory box or our baseball field, means so much more. Their life lives on; even new memories are created. Steven himself wrote a paper about how important it is to keep someone's memory alive. He said, *"Most kids think that a special gift is like an action figure or a stuffed animal. But those are things you buy at a store. The most special gift is something that brings back memories each and every day. A memory brings people back to life for another day just by thinking of it. This is the most special gift of all."*

Holding Steven's physical belongings in our arms, bringing a few of his things on a vacation, buying him a souvenir are small, simple acts which keep

Steven close no matter where we are, no matter what we are doing. One year while in Puerto Rico with some of our family and close family friends, the kids all wrote a huge, "Hi Steven" in the sand. They wanted him to know he was on their minds.

Brianna (far left) and Francesca (second from right) remember Steven on vacation with cousins Vincent, Danielle, and Michael DiBenedetto.

We decided to try to go back to Marco Island, Florida, the spring break after we last were there with Steven. My husband and I were so very hesitant about going back to this familiar locale without our son, but we would be with family friends who would be of enormous comfort no matter where we were, and we knew how much the girls loved going to Marco. We arrived and settled in late in the evening and prepared to officially begin our vacation the next morning. Again, a visitation from Steven entered my dreams.

I was at Deer Path Middle School with some of Steven's best buddies: Bobby, Garrett, Audrey Mardoian, Courtney Galassini, Mykel Vandenberg, Cari Glennon, Brittni

DiTomasso, and assorted other classmates. We decided to come back to our house, and were sitting in our family room when Steven showed up.

Suddenly we all weren't in our family room anymore, but on the beach in Marco Island. Steven asked if I would take some pictures of him with his friends. I began snapping away with my camera. The kids were laughing and hugging on the beach and really hamming it up for the photo op. I then asked if I could take some pictures of Steven alone, because I knew it would be impossible to ever have a new picture of him again. He said "yes," and I was thrilled. Steven's huge smile took over the camera. It was the same wide grin that he had happily worn last year in all of his Marco Island pictures.

Steven was SO happy, and I was in heaven myself for being able to get more photos of my little boy that I thought I wouldn't have a new picture of anymore.

After a long while, Steven told me "I'll be back soon, Mom," and disappeared.

When I woke up in Marco that Sunday morning to begin our trip, I felt peace.

Does a dream or a memory box of souvenirs suddenly make a vacation *great*? No, of course not. Nothing changes our child not being physically with us. What it does do is help keep him with us spiritually, and we choose to bring Steven along wherever we go.

* * *

CHAPTER 24: "GOD, I NEED YOU BACK"

We continued taking the girls to church most Sundays, although I still wasn't sure what "church" meant to me now. I was physically there, but not faithfully. I was still struggling with my relationship with God, asking Him questions, but at least talking to Him all the time now. I'd sit at church, sometimes envisioning Steven's casket in the aisle, trying so hard to remember the dream when he asked me to stop that self-destructive behavior. I'd look over at my husband during Mass and see him holding tightly onto Steven's little batting glove, which Steve now carried everywhere in his pocket but held in his hands at church. Steve always looked so sad in church, sadder than he looked during the week. I wondered why he held the glove so tightly, and why church made him look so much worse. I'd see the kids glazed over during Mass, wondering what was in their heads, wondering if their faith had been spared in all of this.

Since I've been a mother, I prayed the same request to God. Every day. Every night. Every day. Every night. I would ask Him to watch over my children and keep them safe and healthy. My God need never grant me anything but to protect Francesca, Steven and Brianna, and my prayers would be answered. And my beliefs always told me that the God I loved and worshipped would grant this request. I even placed a special decorative plaque at the entrance of my three children's rooms. Steven's plaque read, "*Take a child and watch him grow. Teach him all that he should know. And with our good Lord's help he'll be a kind and gentle man, you'll see.*"

After Steven died, I was just as angry at God as I was at myself. I knew that I was the one who gave Steven the money and the permission to walk to the McDonald's with Garrett that fateful day, but couldn't the God I knew have prevented Steven from being killed? Wasn't the omnipresent, omniscient, omnipotent God that I believed in with every fiber of my being capable of preventing Steven from being hit by the train? I was making headway in so many other aspects of my life, but with regard to my Catholic faith, I was still at a loss. What part did God play in all that was happening in our new world? How could I continue to sit at Mass, trying to keep us going to church, when I no longer knew my faith as I had? I wanted more than to talk to God. I wanted God back, guiding my life.

Down deep, I knew I was still mad at God. I didn't know where to begin the repair this relationship. I spoke to my pastor, Fr. Bill McNulty, at length and during many long, frustrating conversations, posed these questions to him. Where do I go from here? I never asked for much of anything for myself from God. Again and again, I wondered what I had done to deserve this most cruel punishment, and asked Fr. Bill to help me understand.

Fr. Bill would reassure me that Steven's death was not my fault, and was not God's fault, either. He would gently, calmly ask me to be obedient to the mystery, which surrounds earthly tragedy such as this. He would try to reassure me that when I was one day rejoined with Steven and our Lord, I would understand all that I was denied in knowing on this earth. Among it would be the reason why I had lost Steven. I would then gently, calmly tell Fr. Bill that I couldn't wait that long. He would tell me to put the burden of this back onto God, to release the control, the pain and the logic of it, or lack thereof, back into the hands of our Lord. Sometimes he would quietly tell me, "Be gentle with Maria, she needs you." I just couldn't do it. As a mother, I was responsible for the happiness, safety and well being of my children. I could not take a tragedy of this magnitude, any minute change in the events of that day which would have changed the entire outcome, and simply release it to God. I needed some small shred of logic attached to it and until that point, had found none. I didn't realize that looking to your faith for logic was the most complete and utter oxymoron imaginable.

So I sat, and I waited, and I thought long and hard about how I would go on with God still in my life. How could I do more than talk to God and ask Him questions? How could I bring God really, truly back into my life? This was yet another mountain to climb. And I took my time. I let out all my feelings of anger and frustration, and screamed in private to God to ask Him the same questions over and over. *Why did You let this happen? Why didn't You stop Steven? Move his path, slow his walk, turn his head to see the train coming in ample time to keep from being hit? Why is he with You and not me?* I needed answers, I needed meaning, and heaven help me but I needed Steven to give me a sign.

I realized that I also needed God Himself. Even though, for whatever reason, I now needed to live without Steven, I knew that I couldn't live without God in my life. I felt so hopeless at Mass when I used to feel energized and inspired. We had such wonderful priests at St. Pat's, and I always walked away each Sunday with something new to think about and apply to my week. Now I only worried that my inner screams weren't being heard. Didn't God hear me screaming? It was so loud inside of me that the whole world must have known. Who was God to me now? Would I ever know Him again the way I once thought I did?

I thought a lot about analyzing my definition of God, then and now. Would I go on being angry and hurt at the God I thought had let me down by letting Steven get killed? Maybe I was the one who was viewing God in a way that didn't make sense. I not only needed to redefine my relationship with God, I needed to redefine God Himself.

I remember being at Sunday Mass one clear, blue morning, kneeling with the rest of the congregation at St. Pat's, listening to the consecration, the re-enactment of the Last Supper. As the wine chalice was raised and Fr. Larry Hennessy said the words of our Lord, "Do this is remembrance of me," I felt familiar tears stream down my face. I couldn't grasp onto this part of the Lord after losing my child. I couldn't understand the meanings of the teachings that had previously been so embedded in my soul. I knew that Jesus himself offered His life at that Last Supper, but still didn't want to understand why I had to give up my son's life as well. I also remembered that Jesus asked His father to take His cup away, that His life be spared if it was God's will.

As I remained fixated on our priest in those brief moments, the tears continuing, I saw Fr. Hennessy's eyes catch mine. Up at that altar, during that most holy part of our Catholic Mass, as our dear priest and friend looked at me, I saw tears in his eyes as well. Indeed, although there were hundreds of other devoted worshippers there, and I was nowhere near the front pew, Fr. Hennessy felt my pain and met my soul. Our priest, who devoted his life to the mysteries of our faith, cried with me across the church that crisp fall morning. As I reflected on the meaning of that personal moment, I somehow came to a realization of the reaffirmation of God, Jesus and even Father Larry Hennessy. My conclusion that day was that every person, whether it is a mother who lost a child, the leader of a church, even Jesus himself, doesn't face the sacrifice of death with unwavering acceptance. We suffer loss with suffering. This is the fabric of our human existence. We are told to believe that our Lord took the human form over 2,000 years ago to suffer and die for us. Jesus shed His own tears but remained accepting of the fate, which His father bestowed on Him on Good Friday. Knowing that Fr. Larry suffered my fate with me that day at Mass made me want God in my life again, truly back. I wanted to be a believer who believed, not just a follower who stoically attended Mass each week, trying to set the right example for her children but not understanding her faith anymore. I felt like someone began to take a shroud off of my face. A shadow moved away from me that morning as I cried shared tears with Fr. Hennessy.

I started to think of other tragedies in ways I had never examined previously. For instance, in an airplane crash or a suicide bombing, was God letting hundreds of people lose their lives for no reason? Wasn't He able to stop those tragedies as well? Maybe God allowed free will for us on earth, also allowing us to face earthly consequence. Again, I talked to our pastor, Fr. McNulty, who I considered one of my earthly authorities on God. Yes, he believed in free will and that our Lord lets us exercise that free will. But Fr. Bill would also put more reflections in front of me, surely in the hopes that my mind would open beyond the obvious torture I had been putting myself through. He reminded me about Jesus telling the crowds, "Let the little children come to me." He said that our Lord called many to heaven, not just the old and the sick, but the children as well. He also assured me that Jesus only chose the best, and that Steven must have qualified. I cried and knew what he was trying to tell me, that I had no control in this matter, that we are created for a destiny and our Lord has a specific plan for all of us. Fr. McNulty was asking me to release my fear and worries to God, to take this burden off my shoulders.

Fr. McNulty was a man who knew the many faces of Steven. Fr. Bill knew the faithful Steven who served St. Patrick's Church, but he also knew the mischievous Steven who, at the tender age of six, took some black oil-based paint and an old yellow Labrador dog behind the church and painted spots all over him with his good buddy, Tyler, just to have the dog resemble the "101 Dalmatians" movie he had recently seen. Fr. Bill told that very story at Steven's funeral.

Through my search to find the God who defines life, death, and free will for me now, I was most inspired by the words of Elizabeth Edwards, wife of Sen. John Edwards, in her book, "Saving Graces," in which she so eloquently reflects on God and the death of her beloved son, Wade, in a car accident at the age of sixteen. She writes, "*God did not cause our children to die and did not wish them pain or suffering. I came to understand and accept a God willing to stand back and not intervene in accident, disease, violence. It may not be the God we want — certainly it is not the God we now want — but it is the God we have, a God who lets man's actions and the balances of nature take their course whatever the earthly consequences. Where greed or jealousy results in murder, where the lack of moderation results in accidents, when nature is cruel and God does not intervene, we must not be surprised. The causes of grief have always been part of life. The love of God is very different from a protection from tragedy or pain, as perhaps all love, which is so tender, must be. Whether or not our God weeps at man's calamities, I do not know, but I believe in the promise of neither intervention nor protection but only of salvation and enlightenment.*"

I now look at my God in this way. It is, for me and countless other parents who have lost a child or other loved one, the only way in which we can go on in faith. To know that we will see enlightenment on the day we meet our Lord. To know that we cannot attach logic or sense to that which we will never understand, and should not understand. That faith and logic do not coexist in the same worlds. To know that while we are in control of some of our actions, we cannot control every one, nor every step of our child's path. We can know faith if we choose to, whether or not that faith has been tested to this merciless degree. To lose a child is the ultimate test of strength, belief, endurance. To continue living, truly living, is a conscious choice, a rational decision. To continue living in faith, that which is the hardest faith to uphold now, is surely a mountain to climb. But I choose to climb it, knowing that my God would never purposely hurt me, never strip me of my child to punish me for some past transgression. This understanding and re-evaluation of God in my life has moved me onward to continue the Christian life I led before Steven's death. This path of personal reflection has enriched my life beyond seeking the immediate answers I needed because of Steven's death. It is only when I truly forgave God that I was able to begin to forgive myself.
The fragmentation between us began to heal, and because of it, my own inner and outer self joined again.

Sharing our pain with the spiritual leaders of our church, our priests, and listening to their reflections, re-opened doors to my personal faith. This re-examination of my religious belief system is just one of the many ways in which I have delved into deeper layers of meaning in my life, of finding new texture, new pattern in the fabric of my being.

By redefining God in my life, I was able to go back to God. He, my God, lets us act in earthly ways, which include earthly consequence. He welcomes the believers into His divine kingdom no matter what journey they take to get there. My little boy walked the path of a child drawn to our Lord in his life, and was surely embraced by our Lord in his death. Did my God really change?

Of course not. Did I change? Absolutely. Although the dark, earthly truth of Steven's death will never change, I will trust in the light, which led him home.

V.A. Storey writes, *"Oh God, make me brave for life. Oh, braver than this. Let me straighten after pain, as a tree straightens after the rain, shining and lovely again. God, make me brave for life, much braver than this. As the bloom grass lifts, let me rise from sorrow with quiet eyes, knowing Thy way is wise. God, make me brave. Life brings such blinding things. Help me to keep my sight, help me to see aright. That out of darkness comes light."*

* * *

CHAPTER 25: HOLIDAYS WITH STEVEN

I remember staring out the living room window one night in early December, 2003. The windy snow outside was blowing positively sideways. One sure bet in Chicago during any season of the year is that any and all weather conditions are accompanied by wind. Rain, leaves, and snow are gravity-challenged by the gusts in Chicago. I sat mesmerized at the swirling winds as they created this slanted snowstorm. I pitied the barren trees, the branches huddled together so tightly, the wind knotting them this way and that, as torturous blasts of wind and snow repeatedly tested their endurance.

As we approached that first Christmas without Steven, we were also approaching eight months without him. This holiday would be the ultimate test of our endurance, and we'd surely need to huddle together. My husband and I wished we could spring forward from Halloween to January 1, 2004. We thought long and hard about going away for the holidays, which would give us reprieve from decorating, cooking, baking, socializing and otherwise acknowledging this "magical" time of year, and just magically disappear. The holidays could happen while we were gone. Would that be so bad? After all, we couldn't imagine decorating our tree with ornaments when some of the ornaments were ones Steven had made in school, wrapping presents for our children without Steven's name on a third of them, baking cookies without Steven there to enjoy his favorite Italian style lemon knots, sending a family Christmas card without Steven's picture and name on it. I also would be turning 40 on the day after Christmas that year. All thoughts of celebration felt unwelcome and unneeded. Every aspect of this holiday season just seemed wrong.

However, to our extended family, what seemed "right" was to have us home and to all be together, at least through Christmas itself. In hindsight, even our two daughters really wouldn't have understood Christmas not happening here at home. They were both young, and our then nine year-old, Brianna, believed in Santa Claus, and not having Santa leave her presents felt selfish on our part. When we still gave the girls their Easter gifts and treats the morning after Steven was killed, it was done purely in a state of shock and also because the presents were already there, waiting to be given. Easter had been planned out and purchased. Now we'd have to consciously make Christmas a reality.

I thought about what could be done to sidestep some of our traditional customs to make them a little more palatable that year. We didn't have to create the exact Christmas we usually did in order for it to qualify as "Christmas." Our Christmas had always been celebrated in a big way. This was definitely a year we needed to "simplify." I looked at each of our rituals as individual parts of a whole and evaluated which were essential, which could be eliminated, and which could be merely toned down for this difficult first year without Steven. For us, Christmas didn't need to happen. For the girls, it had to.

I started out this process with thinking about how I could possibly send a Christmas card. I realized that my old-fashioned upbringing would call this first year my "mourning period" and etiquette would say that I shouldn't send a Christmas card at all. Along with not wearing black, I decided not to worry about this breach of protocol, either. Being a typical American mom, each year I followed the tradition of sending a photo card with our three children's happy, smiling faces gracing the front. However, this year, there could be no card with just the two girls together. There could be no message of "rejoice" or "celebrate." There were no smiling faces to be had, Christmas time or otherwise. And we had already begun receiving thought-filled cards by the armloads that year — even before Thanksgiving. I thought long and hard about what could be sent out that was both appropriate in representing the deep and reflective feelings of our family, and what would acknowledge the abundance of support and sentiment that was being sent our way — yet again.

I fashioned a message myself and laid it out at our local printer, a shop called "Alphagraphics" in Bannockburn, IL, basically the next town over to Lake Forest. Alphagraphics had also printed our "thank-you" note and I trusted them with this next most personal task for us.

I took the letters of Steven's name and lined them up vertically along the left margin of a plain ivory card. We had the letters to Steven's name printed in gold foil, glittering and aligned along the left side of the card, and made sure we had a beautiful gold foil halo over his name as it was now part of our family signature and always would be. We received upwards of 500 Christmas cards that year, and kept them all in appreciation of everyone who reached out to us.

Seasons like this bring us moments
To give thanks for our blessings,
Embrace those around us,
Value our time together, and
Envision the return of peace in our
New Year.

Love from the Malins ~

Steve, Maria, Francesca, Steven, & Brianna

Decorating our home for Christmas was like taking a trip down the memory lane of our family, and was extremely painful for all four of us. We opened the boxes of decorations; three Christmas stockings to hang on our fireplace mantle, three choir angels to place in our front yard, three grapevine reindeer to display by our front door. We unconsciously lived our lives in "three's", and the sight of the trios of Christmas decorations was another painful reminder that now there were only "two." Still, we knew it was the right thing to do to put out the three of everything we had. In fact, we knew back then that we might never be able to reduce our Christmas decorations and, in hindsight, we haven't. Steven's stocking will hang on our mantle each and every holiday. We can't say "good-bye" to the stocking, or any of the other decorations. Having the three of everything still reminds us that we will always have three children — one of them now just celebrates in heaven.

When it came to hanging the ornaments on the kid's Christmas tree, which had traditionally displayed all the ones they made in school over the years, we had a problem. We found it too painful to touch and hold all those arts-and-crafts ornaments so lovingly made by our children, and decided not to put up a "kid's tree" that year. Now, holding the ornaments made by Steven and remembering his age when he made each one brings us comfort. That first year, it was far too much to bear.

I sat down next to the Christmas tree one evening, staring at the Nativity scene that my great Aunt Lucy had given to my husband and me at our bridal shower in 1987. I thought about the years that the kids each fought to place the baby Jesus on the manger, the final touch in putting together the Nativity each holiday. Nobody fought for the baby Jesus this year; I just placed Him in the manger myself. I stared at Mary and Joseph looking protectively over the swaddled infant Jesus, and wondered about this tender moment. I then reflected on the violent death of Jesus at the Crucifixion. We so fiercely guard the well being and safety of our precious babies. When they die a violent death, what happens to the gentle innocence of those moments? How do we remember the swaddled infant without remembering the look of death on their beautiful young face?

I had received a small Pieta statue from a dear family friend named Madeline Parisi, who was living in Rome for a few years, and found myself that first year wanting to change out the protected infant Jesus in the manger with the lifeless body of Jesus in Mary's arms, having just been taken off the cross. I didn't have my protected baby Steven anymore, only the lifeless body of my son in the emergency room. The Pieta would have represented my child more accurately under the Christmas tree that year. Nothing felt innocent, nothing felt gentle and protected. Death hung over my shoulder as I continued to stare at the manger. How was I going to take "death" out of this Christmas and bring back birth and life? I needed to find more ways to keep the "alive" Steven with us for the holiday. I was exhausted from the effort, but knew it was right to at least try. *I'm trying for you, Steven, and because your sisters so need Christmas. This is so unfair to them. Be with us. Yes, God, I know You're there, too.*

The thought of buying gifts for the kids was not only tough for us, but also hard on the girls. They had always bought a little something or crafted a homemade gift for each other for Christmas, and we encouraged this custom because it reinforced an important message that we not only receive, we somehow give, no matter what our age. The holidays weren't only about the joy of gifts being received, but about the joy of giving itself. But in the nucleus of our little family, there it was, that big, gaping hole. One major person could no longer give and no longer receive. This void could not be filled, and neither Steve nor I knew what to do about it. In fact, the whole tradition of brightly colored holiday paper glittering under our tree felt wrong. Gifts in holiday colors didn't mirror our sad holiday moods. No presents for or from Steven seemed empty and cruel. Again, we felt the pain of this tremendous loss in our lives. I quieted myself and listened and looked around, and asked for a sign. I wanted to count a blessing. I needed to feel the life of my son infused into this holiday. My hope in Steven's continued presence in my life helped an idea materialize, and gave me the inspiration to finish making Christmas happen.

Some of the physical possessions Steven left behind were gift cards. It had become common, his last few birthdays, to receive small gift cards to purchase a video game or movie. It was a practice that his middle school-aged friends all seemed to be doing, partly due to the ease of it, partly because the gift recipient could then pick out the gift of his or her choice. He would receive gift cards for birthdays, and had several from his birthday that had just passed, to stores such as Best Buy and Blockbuster Video, which would have been saved and used for the special purchase of a video game or new computer accessory. So, I had all these gift cards, and no Steven to buy anything for. I decided that I'd split up the dollar amounts from them and begin buying small gifts for the girls from their brother. These gift cards lasted far beyond that holiday, but a few of these were used that first Christmas. Now, there would be gifts under the tree "from Steven" for his sisters, and it truly felt to all of us like they came from him. I decided against Christmas wrapping paper, as it did just feel too festive. I realized that gifts needed to be wrapped, but this year they wouldn't be in holiday theme. So, simple, unadorned wrapping paper cloaked our gifts under the tree, a nod to our solemn moods, a respect for the lack of celebration that this year warranted.

I also took the opportunity to frame some of Steven's last artwork, school papers and some of the memorial tributes given to us on his behalf, and also placed them under the tree for the girls and my husband to open. The framed gifts all said, "To Steven," and my family was baffled at first to see the gifts with his name on them. However, when they began opening, they realized that these were actually gifts that Steven had given to us before he left this earth — his reflections on life at age eleven, his school paper on heroes, his "top ten reasons to be thankful" from the Christmas before — all opened and appreciated for their inspiration and opportunity for our family to stop and reflect on Steven. Seeing these Steven mementos all together also reminded me of the gentle, wonderful boy so full of life, thoughts and dreams. It served to re-create the image of life I needed to feel at least a little invested in Christmas itself. It re-created the image of my "alive" son.

We also watched the video of our last Christmas together, that of 2002, on Christmas Eve day. Seeing Steven's face so excited to see new air hockey and foosball games in the basement, him patiently waiting his turn to open his gifts, our three kids joking with each other, the bliss of Christmas morning for a family who didn't know that it would be their last as a family of five.

Today, we still need to incorporate our son and brother into important events like Christmas. Our front hall table is adorned with framed photos of our past Christmas cards when the three kids were together. The girls love to look at them each year.

We talk of Steven as we make the lemon knot cookies as a family; we still laugh about him being able to put away dozens of clams and mussels. We buy an extra gift for Frankie and Bri from Steven each year. We have Christmas Eve Mass said in his name. Whenever there's an opportunity to add something meaningful to our Christmas that will be a symbol of our three children, we do so. I've heard of an extended family that pulls names for a grab bag, and when someone picks the name of the young cousin who has gone to heaven, they donate a small sum to charity in that family member's name.

We try to incorporate some message of this journey in our Christmas card each year to reflect on how we have, indeed, moved forward as a family and of course, include Steven's name with the halo over it.

The first Christmas in the new house, I surprised my husband with a chalk sketch of our three kids done by an artist who had drawn the airline employees who lost their lives on 9/11. The artist's name was Sally Baker Keller, a local from a Northern suburb of Chicago. I asked her to draw our children at a slightly older age than the ages when we lost Steven; more at 16, 13 and 11 than 13, 11 and 9. Steven would be in between the girls with his arms protectively around them, and I had even given Sally a favorite shirt from each of the kids to use as their clothing. The portrait graces the front entry of our home, and this gift to my husband helped make our son a very present member of our new home, not to mention our second holiday without him.

Last year, I was so proud of Brianna, who gave us each a most wonderful homemade surprise Christmas gift, even one for Steven. We had come home on Christmas Eve night and Brianna was begging us to open the gifts she made for us. We usually waited to open family gifts until the morning, but she was on a mission and wouldn't/couldn't wait. She sat us all down on the couch and, with a handful of papers, began to read each of us a poem she had either found online or written herself. The poems were tailored to what her relationship was with each of us, mother, father, sister. Steven's was about a guardian angel watching over her, and we cried as we listened.

To Francesca, Brianna read in part: *"No matter what happens to me or to you, we will always make it through because we will always be SISTERS FOREVER."*

To my husband, Brianna said: *"You may have thought I didn't see, or that I hadn't heard, life lessons that you taught to me but I got every word."*

To me, she said: *"You're my dependable source of comfort, my cushion when I fall. You help me in times of trouble; you support me whenever I call."*

And finally, to her big brother, her guardian angel, Brianna read: *"There's an invisible angel that watches over us. He's always there, one that we can trust. Wears the whitest of white, just like a dove. Comes down to protect us, from Heaven above. His wings are magnificent, as big as the sky. His halo is shining, a gold no one can buy. He shows us the good and guides us from the bad. He is no longer with us, but don't be sad. We love him no matter what, we'll remember his laughter. We will remember the good things that he left after."*

Brianna then handed each of us a CD she burned with our favorite songs. Steven got one, too. Although we all sat in tears, they were once again filled with the water of life. I was jubilant with pride knowing that Brianna "got it," knew what the true meaning of family was, and remembered her brother with the rest of us for Christmas. Outside our kitchen door that night stood the first deer we saw in our yard since moving to the new home. I was sure it was a sign from Steven that he was looking in, watching us, symbolically there like Santa's reindeer bringing Christmas to all who believed in it still. We knew we did.

No, we didn't have Christmas cookies that first year or sparkly wrapping paper, but Christmas did return each year thereafter, and with it, Steven has joined us each time.

* * *

CHAPTER 26: A HOLY WEEK

Indeed, Christmas comes every year. The tides of the seasons and holidays and life's annual celebrations continue to rise up to our shore and greet us. Whether we are ready for each event or holiday, they come, again and again. We consciously prepare ourselves now for just about every occasion, whether it's Christmas, a birthday, or Easter. Especially Easter. We want to feel prepared ahead of the event so that we can peacefully greet it. We want to calmly welcome life in our new world, continuing its ebbs and tides, especially its rituals. We still struggle with Easter, and probably always will.

Each year, as we mark the beginning of Lent on Ash Wednesday, we begin the annual Christian ritual of sacrifice and for us, know we are approaching the milestone of another year without Steven. We reflect on the life of Jesus Christ as he was tempted by the devil in the desert, and we abstain and pray during the forty days of Lent. We remember the ultimate sacrifice of our Lord, and can't help but mirror those feelings of loss as we approach Holy Week and the anniversary of Steven's death.

Holy Week, which marks the journey of the Passion, crucifixion and resurrection of Jesus, is filled with symbolism for me. Steven's death on Holy Saturday takes me on an introspective path each year, in which I deeply reflect on the human life of our Lord, the life and faith of my young child, and my own faith. I find great meaning in Holy Week, and feel it is not only a time to embrace and relive the days of the last week of my son's life, but the symbolism of the sacrifice of the only Son of God. While I cannot say that I find comfort in this annual journey, I now find myself particularly close to my faith at this time each year, and always find new layers of meaning beneath my son's death and the death of our Lord.

From a tender age, Steven was a child of immense faith. He privately expressed his awe at the exemplary life of Jesus, and outwardly exhibited great curiosity with religious icons and symbolism. He collected saint statues and religious medals and holy cards from various services we attended over the years. He proudly displayed messages in his room, which said, "I believe in Jesus." He was a child of faith and worship beyond his young years, a boy who saw depth of meaning beyond the surface teachings of Catholicism.

I had an interesting conversation with Steven during Holy Week, the last week of his young life, where he was reflecting on something he had learned in CCD class at church. Steven had especially loved the hymn, "Jesus, Remember Me" when it was sung at his great aunt's funeral a few years before, but never understood the meaning behind the words, "*Jesus, remember me, when I come into Your kingdom.*" He only knew that he loved the verse, and hummed it over and over after the service. On his last day of CCD that week, he came home with two pieces of exciting news. The first was that he was tied for perfect CCD attendance for the year with a fellow student, a sweet little girl named Sarah Jaekel. The other news was that he finally understood the meaning behind the hymn, "Jesus, Remember Me." His teacher, Mrs. Mary Ellen Alt, a wonderful religious education teacher for many years at St. Pat's, had taught the children that day about the criminals who hung on the crosses on either side of Jesus, and about the one criminal who had repented and asked Jesus for forgiveness, asking our Lord to allow him to enter into His kingdom of heaven that night after his death. "*Jesus, remember me, when I come into Your kingdom.*" Steven came home so happy, having been enlightened into the true meaning of this favorite hymn. I remember him saying over and over, "I get it now, Mom. I finally get it." To this day, I don't remember why I had not taught Steven the meaning of the hymn myself, and wonder why it took a religious education instructor a few days before my son's death to bring him to its true meaning. Perhaps it is true what is said that when our work on this earth is done, when we "get it," no matter what the age, then it is time to go home to the Lord. *But I wanted your home to always be here with me.*

Two days before his death, Steven was asked to serve Holy Thursday Mass and assist our pastor in the symbolic "washing of the disciples' feet" by Jesus at the Last Supper. Six members of our parish had been chosen to have their feet washed, all people who were honored because of their volunteerism to our church and devotion to their faith. Steven solemnly held a stack of white towels, which were used to dry the feet, assisting Fr. McNulty as he knelt before each recipient of this rite of the Last Supper. Later in the service, Steven held the water and wine as the consecration was prepared. Steven proudly rang the small hand-held bell for the "Glory to God." I was extremely proud of him that night. His service to our Catholic faith meant a great deal to me. In hindsight, the fact that Steven participated in this important ritual of Holy Week, just two days before his own calling, holds great symbolism for me to this day, making me feel as though Steven was somehow "chosen" to closely walk the path of Jesus, to wash the feet, to help with the preparation of the consecration, to ring the bell of an angel, or soon-to-be angel.

My husband, Steve, and I refer to Good Friday, the last day of Steven's life, as "Great Friday" because it was an especially wonderful day for our son. While his Holy Thursday participation was so symbolic for me, the events of Steven's Good Friday brought great happiness to my husband.

The day began with a father and son Easter haircut, their three week ritual which kept Steven's buzz cut ever the short length. After a quick shower at home, Steve and Steven, Jr. invited our dear family friend and close buddy of Steven's, Nicholas Childs, to attend a college baseball game together. They loved spending an afternoon in their favorite company watching their favorite sport. I took our daughters shopping for the afternoon for shoes and dresses for Francesca's Confirmation the next week, while the boys reveled in hours of baseball.

Steven got home just in time to gobble down some of his favorite fried shrimp from a local pizzeria and head out again for an evening pitching-and-catching baseball clinic near our home. My husband and son came home with huge smiles as Steven's performance at the clinic and good sportsmanship earned him lots of praise with the coaches who led the program.

So, although there was no direct religious connection to Steven's last day on this earth, we think of Great Friday as our child spending his last hours with us enjoying what he loved most in life — laughter, quality time with family and friends, and baseball.

And then on Holy Saturday, Steven, like the souls of purgatory, was lifted up by the Lord and carried home. We were not ready for him to leave. We had not packed his bags, only his Easter basket for the next morning. What parent is ever ready to send their child home to another place? Home is here, under our roof. Within the safety of our own care. We did not finish Holy Week that year with an egg hunt and Easter Mass and a big family celebration. We said good-bye to our only son, much as God sacrificed His only son for us. And so each year, Holy Week brings me back to the week in 2003 when meanings were unveiled, journeys were walked, the Last Supper was re-enacted, and even much baseball was played. And the ultimate sacrifice was asked of us.

A letter sent to us from one of the coaches of the baseball clinic sponsored by "Full Package Athletics" that Good Friday evening is something we will always cherish. His praise of Steven meant so much. It truly was Stevie's *Great* Friday.

Dear Mr. and Mrs. Malin,

"Please forgive me if any of the following furthers your pain in any way. My name is Marty Patterson, and I was fortunate enough to spend two hours with your son on Friday evening, April 18.

With every camp and clinic that Todd Fine and I perform, thereafter, we always discuss the success of the camp or clinic. Within these discussions, the young man whom we most enjoyed is always revealed. That Friday night, there wasn't a hint of hesitation amongst Todd or I over who illuminated the pitching and catching clinic. Your son uniquely did.

As you know, as a coach, you strive not to have a 'favorite,' you try not to disclose your partiality towards a young man; but it is often inevitable. A coach's partiality is not based on talent alone, but on that special young man's character, respect, and desire. Friday night's 'favorite,' your son, distinctly displayed each of these attributes over the course of the clinic.

On April 18, because the majority of the kids expressed their interest in pitching, Todd gave everyone a brief pitching demonstration. As the kids lined up to play catch, I chose not to walk around the gym and analyze the other kids' technique, like I normally do. I, instead, chose to stand in the Northwest corner of the gym. Near me, a fresh-faced young man threw a ball that the catcher couldn't even see — in fact, the catcher didn't raise his glove until after the ball had already ricocheted off the wall. I looked at your son. . .he flashed that broad, beaming smile. The inevitable happened; I would no longer be able to conceal my favoritism.

The clinic had reached the point where the catchers and pitchers would now separate into two different groups. When the kids were asked if they were pitchers or catchers, your son declared himself a catcher. After having seen him throw the ball so swiftly, I unfairly said to him, 'Are you sure that you aren't a pitcher?' He shyly looked at me but sternly said, 'Yes, I am a catcher.' He certainly was, and the heart that your boy displayed, it caught my heart. I hope that he knew.

Your son's courage, passion, attentiveness, politeness and delightful personality moved me profoundly. It was truly an honor to have had your son participate in our camps. Full Package Athletics will forever miss, and never forget, his fervor and charm, which complemented that youthful smile of his so very well.

Although time unfairly and too early chose a different destiny for Steven, he had already developed into an exemplary young man, well beyond his years. You and Mrs. Malin taught that boy very well.

Mr. and Mrs. Malin, on behalf of Full Package Athletics, Inc., I send you and your family our deepest condolences and, because your son made such a gleaming impression by so well exemplifying the precise character in a young man for which we wish all our student athletes to have, we request your permission to give us the honor of naming the annual pitching and catching clinic after your son."

With sympathy,

Marty Patterson

Full Package Athletics

* * *

CHAPTER 27: STEVEN, BE WITH US

A few weeks before Francesca left for her first year of college, we decided to take a family vacation. It was early August, 2007, and we thought that a few days away would bring some quality time for the four of us before she began her freshman year. The usual feelings of longing for Steven's presence were there, and for me, they were combined with a new grief over our first child going away to college. Brianna would now truly be without a sibling at home, and the worry over her possible sadness, the loss of another one of our children being physically at home, and the overall change in our family dynamic were causing me considerable stress.

We decided to venture to the East coast, and headed for a few relaxing days in Cape Cod, followed by a few days of shopping and sightseeing in Boston. As we sat on the runway waiting to take off from O'Hare Airport in Chicago, I felt like a clock inside me was ticking away, counting down the minutes until our family at home would soon whittle down to a sad three. I almost didn't want to go on the vacation, instead wanting to run up to my room and bury my head under the covers, not wanting to face another impending feeling of doom, not wanting to face still another facet of my new world, not wanting to lose the daily physical connection to another of my children. The day-to-day challenges of life as a family of four were enough, and now another child would soon be gone. Although I knew that the leave was for a positive reason, it felt, to me, like "loss" nevertheless. I felt selfish due to these thoughts, and I knew it would be unfair of me to share them with Frankie. Was our daughter's departure for college going to be like falling off another cliff? This time, we knew the cliff was coming, that we were inching toward the day a few short weeks away when our steps would once again lead us to a fall. What would happen to life inside our home with Francesca away at school? Her life in high school with cheerleading and friends and just general daily news was a pulse at our dinner table each night, and the foreboding quiet with just Bri at home would be difficult on us all.

Then there were the usual conversations with other parents whose children were also embarking on their first college year. "Oh wow, you guys are almost empty nesters! How exciting is that?" I wanted to scream, "I'd give both my arms and legs to have my three children with me forever and ever!" They'd say, "Brianna will be an only child." I wanted to scream, "Brianna shouldn't be an only child! She should still have her older brother with her. This is fate at its worst. How dare you make such insensitive comments?" Instead, I said nothing. I'd smile, nod and change the subject to the topic of their lives. I guess I really had mastered this conversation-switch thing. *Yes, we'll keep the topics on you so you don't have the chance to tell us how "lucky" we are.*

I kept trying to tell myself that I was overreacting about Frankie leaving for school, that this was a natural course in life. That I should only have feelings of happiness for her. That I needed to keep it together for my family. I knew it would be up to us to help fill the void for Brianna. I would try to help make sure that she was well-occupied while her sister was away. More sleepovers. More inviting her friends to join us on family outings. More trying to connect with Bri and be part of her life. Not so easy with a thirteen year-old, but I would try.

I was so worked up over my overlapping emotions that I knew it would be next to impossible for me to relax on this East coast vacation. For the beginning of the week we were away, my emotions ran wild. My daughters' usual sibling bickering sent me reeling. Didn't they realize another cliff was coming? Didn't they know they should cherish every moment together because they'd soon be apart for months? We'd be sightseeing and Frankie would express how excited she was to leave for school. I'd make sure my sunglasses hid my tears. I'd spend my private moments on the vacation crying over unwelcome grief, worrying over unwelcome loss. My family didn't know how to deal with a wife and mother so out of sorts. It was not the best start to a vacation, in large part due to me.

In my quietest moments, I asked Steven to help us get through the vacation, to help me calm down. And help me, he did. His presence erupted everywhere on the trip, signs and symbols cropping up wherever we turned. It took a bit to open myself up to allow the joy from them.

We checked in at the car rental agency at Boston Logan, and on a busy Friday afternoon, the place was total chaos. We would be driving from Boston to the Cape that afternoon, sure to hit miles of "weekend getaway" traffic from the city. I'd ordered our rental car with a GPS navigational system, knowing from past trips that co-piloting was not one of my husband and my stronger suits, and was disappointed to find out that the last car with GPS had already been checked out that day. We tried to upgrade to another car, even downsize to a car with GPS that might fit our luggage, but nothing worked. With no options left, no prior experience on driving to Cape Cod, and little talent when it comes to new directions, my husband and I solemnly left the rental counter to begin loading our bags into the car. All of a sudden, what drives up but an SUV being returned with, what else, a GPS? We looked at each other, and at the agent who was kind enough to eagerly radio for the car to be cleaned up immediately. Our son, who sat in the back seat with his sisters during countless trips to the Wisconsin Dells or Disney World, patiently waiting for his parents to re-navigate and find their way to a destination, knew that we desperately needed a GPS in our rental car. And Steven surely made certain that we got it that chaotic Friday afternoon in Boston. I looked up, clasped my hands, and of course, cried.

Saturday, the first full day of our vacation, found us spending a gloomy, humid, rainy day browsing the tourist and souvenir shops in downtown Chatham, Massachusetts. It was a lackluster way to begin the trip, and we all were a little disappointed. I knew the kids were eager to get out and enjoy the beautiful resort pool, and the sun would have brightened the mood all around. Late in the afternoon, we returned to the hotel to watch a little TV and read.

I stepped outside to the balcony of our room and found myself having another good cry. We were sharing a room with the kids, and there was no immediate place for solitude or to release the pent-up feelings I'd been experiencing. The weather had not cleared up enough to support a walk around the resort property. As I stood with my chin resting on my hands, I stared at the beautiful scenery of the Lower Cape, consumed with self-pity, hating myself for the feelings I couldn't suppress. Out of nowhere, two tiny yellow birds flew past our hotel balcony. The birds surprised me as they had so many times before, but especially in this different locale. Were these birds finches? I didn't even care. They flew past again, and I took it as a sign telling me that Steven was close by, wanting me to dry my tears, get myself together and head inside to my family. The sign from my son was, as usual, sent at the perfect moment, and luckily for me, I was open enough to take it as a symbol of the nearness of my beloved child. I wiped my face and thanked Steven, heading back inside the room to watch some television with Steve and the girls.

We took the girls go-carting that Sunday night, and though reluctant, I decided to accept my daughters' invitation to get my own cart and join them in the fun. I had not go-carted in a very long time; probably for more than eight years. We found ourselves at the end of a very long line of people waiting their turn, and I knew we'd be there a while. We watched groups being called in sets of two or four, and expected to wait several rounds before we got to take our turn. Within a few minutes, we unexpectedly heard a call for a group of "three." Although we were a group of three, we were sure that someone ahead of us in that long line would take the open spot. No one did! Happily, the girls and I ran to the front of the line and snagged the last three go-carts on the starting track. There was no time to really put any thought into selecting a cart or anything; we just the enjoyed the sheer luck of being called so quickly and took our turn. My cart was light blue, Steven's favorite color of his favorite North Carolina basketball team, although I made no connection to it in that hastened moment. I jumped in and away we all sped around the track. My husband watched from the side and I saw him motion a "number one" and a "number three" with his fingers, but was going too fast to really pay attention to it. The go-carting was a great treat in light of the choppy start the trip had. When we pulled in the carts, the girls and Steve started yelling to me, "Number 13! You had cart number 13!" What were the chances that we would get to go ahead of an extremely long waiting line, that I would get a light blue cart, and that it would be number13? The only chance of all that happening at once was that it was Steven sending us another sign. Was it really the reason that all of it happened? To me, to all of us, definitely yes. It was the meaning we attached to this and so many other occurrences on this trip, making us feel the presence of our son and brother as we traveled through another journey, him spiritually along, if not physically.

Our drive back to Boston on Tuesday to spend the second half of our trip held a few surprises as well. As we headed down Highway 6 toward the city, we passed a large water tank in one of the towns. A beautiful rainbow had been painted on it. Again, a sign from Steven. When we walked the Freedom Trail in Boston, we kept passing a Jack Daniel's Whiskey delivery truck. Jack Daniel's is and always has been my husband's cocktail-of-choice, and we took the repeated appearance of the truck on the streets we walked as a funny little sign from Steven to his dad. Did we have to attribute the sighting of a delivery truck to being a sign from our son? Of course not. Still, it added to the joy of the day to think that Steven was trying to say "hello" to us, giggling with his dad, and helping us know that he was close by that day.

We experienced the most signs from Steven on the last day of our trip. The day was filled with Steven, and it created special memories for all of us of that last vacation before Francesca's college years began.

It was Wednesday, the day before we were to fly home to Chicago, and we decided to spend the day shopping and sightseeing. We started our morning with a run to the local Starbuck's near our hotel. I'm not a big coffee drinker, and had already had a small cup in our room, so I decided to wait outside Starbuck's and watch the foot traffic go by as my family got their beverages. The kids really wanted me to order something, even a cold drink, and Brianna begged me to try a Starbuck's raspberry lemonade. I am not a fan of raspberry-flavored anything, so I declined. The three of them, my husband and the girls, were in the Starbuck's for around fifteen minutes when Brianna came running out with a raspberry lemonade in hand. I asked her why she had ordered it for me after all, and she said that she hadn't. Someone else ordered it and the clerk made two by mistake, and so they asked if anyone wanted to try a "free" raspberry lemonade. Brianna immediately thought of me, accepted the drink and ran outside with it. Again, we took this as a sign that Steven as well as Bri really wanted me to try that lemonade!

We stopped for lunch at an outdoor café on Newberry Street, and all week long Brianna had been having a taste for her favorite pasta dish with light marinara sauce and shrimp. However, no matter where we ate, including Little Italy on the North End of Boston, we couldn't seem to find the exact entrée she'd had such a taste for. We chose a cozy Newberry Street café mainly because it had the closest thing to her pasta dish, just without the shrimp, and decided to eat there. We placed our orders and waited for lunch to arrive, Brianna anticipating her pasta. When the meal arrived, we were again shocked to see that a little something had arrived on the plate that we had not ordered. Mixed in with the delicious pasta was shrimp! Did we look at the menu incorrectly? We knew that a restaurant could never choose to include something as allergic as shellfish with an entrée as a surprise. We also knew that when we perused the menu before we chose to go into that restaurant, we did not see shrimp as part of that item. But magically, the exact meal that Brianna had been wanting all week was presented as if from heaven above. To us, it was another sign from our little boy, making sure that his little sister had the lunch she so desired.

As we ate, we talked about the unexpected situation and all the signs from Steven that week, when we noticed that the building next to the rear of the restaurant had graffiti on it. Not surprising for an urban locale like Boston, right? We noticed that the graffiti word started with the letter "S," so we decided to get up and take a closer look at it. As we did so, we weren't surprised that it appeared to be written for us alone. The "S" began the word, "Sweet," which was one of Steven's favorite adjectives in the whole world. "Sweeeet" was used to describe anything that caused supreme happiness in the life of our vivacious 11 year-old child. So, to us, that magical graffiti which graced the wall of that magical building where we enjoyed that magical lunch that last day of our vacation was sent by none other than our supremely sweeeet and magical son and brother, just to make sure that we knew he was close by in heart and soul.

In the end, the trip, with all the signs and symbols from Steven, was anything but sad and stressful. We found ourselves in the best sightseeing locale we had been to thus far, and many profoundly wonderful sights were sent to us from Steven himself.

* * *

CHAPTER 28: IT TAKES A COMMUNITY

Hillary Clinton quoted the famous, *"It takes a village..."* For our family, it took a community. From the first moments of this nightmare to today, our uniquely caring community has helped to see us through. Folks who had simply been good neighbors and fellow parents stepped up in momentous ways to reach out to us in support. And their support was our anti-depressant. Their concern was the constant, burning light in this dark tunnel, helping us, guiding us through so that we were never alone in the darkness. Lake Forest is unique in the level of care and concern offered to those in our community who need assistance, whatever the situation. Our fellow residents step in and organize dinner rotations, take over carpools, run errands, drive the elderly to doctor's appointments, help raise funds for a family in need of costly medical care; the list goes on and on. Our situation brought out the best in good deeds from so many people. I wish they could see how wonderful they were and still are in our eyes. I wish they could feel the love that we've felt from them. I wish I could say thank-you over and over, and give back the strength of the hugs and the power of the prayer that we've received from so many that I'm proud to call neighbors and friends.

Francesca came home from school on Steven's first anniversary in heaven, on April 19, 2004. She wore a white ribbon on her sweater. When I asked what the white ribbon was for, she burst into tears. A few of her childhood friends, wonderful girls like Ashley Tomanek and Elizabeth Crawford, had hand made and passed out hundreds of white ribbons for the high school students to wear in remembrance of Steven's anniversary. The kids didn't have to say a word. With a dignified quiet about them, they simply wore the ribbons to let Francesca know that she was being thought of that day, and offered her hugs whenever possible. Every year of Francesca's years at Lake

Forest High School were marked with her peers wearing white ribbons on April 19th to remember her little brother and keep him close that day. There are no words to describe the profound feeling of care and concern this gave our daughter and our family. This was and still is a bright light in our tunnel.

Our dear family friend who is also a freelance writer, Conrad Theodore, honored Steven on his one-year anniversary in heaven by writing an article, complete with Steven's photo, in "North Shore" magazine, a monthly publication well-known in Chicago. The piece was entitled, "Remembering Steven — One Year Later," and was so thoughtfully written and captured Steven's spirit so beautifully that it gave our family tremendous comfort. For me personally with my writing, Conrad has been a frequent source of encouragement as well objectivity these past few years, and I can't thank him enough for all of his support.

About a year after my essay on the baseball tournament rainbow was published in our local paper, I had the opportunity to interview for and provide some writing samples to that same newspaper who was now looking to fill a spot for a weekly columnist. It was Conrad who talked it through with me, being the first to congratulate me when I secured the position. I will be forever grateful for his guidance in my writing, and more importantly, for his friendship to my family.

I realized that while watching Steven play baseball all those years, I didn't take enough pictures or video of him. Among so many other regrets, I felt that I didn't have enough photos of our little boy playing the game he loved so much. Fellow baseball parents began stepping forward in numbers to offer any photo they had of Steven with their child, any footage of Steven playing. Friends of ours, Ross and Nancy Friedman, had a wonderful picture of Steven in his catcher's uniform, leaning against the fence at the end of a game. I took this candid shot of him and had it blown up to a large poster size. I wrapped it and gave it to my husband for Father's Day on year. It proudly hangs in our basement on Steven's wall of sports, where I've also framed his football and basketball uniforms for my husband.

So many wonderful, caring people sent me guardian angel mementos after Steven's death. Mostly, I received angel pins, and, at the beginning, I wore them every day. I had small guardian angels to wear, cherub-like and delicate, and large angel pins that were heavy and cumbersome on my clothing, often putting little holes in my shirt or sweater. But I wore them all. I wore them as my badge of courage every day. Even on the days that I wasn't sure of anything, and there were hundreds of those, I wore my guardian angels, imagining Steven on my shoulder. At those times, I wore them purely to give me strength to get through the day, symbolically keeping Steven close to my heart.

I lost a few of the pins amidst the chaos of those first months, the backing coming off unbeknownst to me, and I would cry over the loss. Each pin was a gift from someone who cared about us, and any loss of those precious gifts was difficult. The pins reminded me of so many who put forth effort to bring comfort to my family and me.

I wear Steven's watch daily, even today. It's a stainless steel Seiko watch, one we had given him on his First Holy Communion on May 7, 2000. I found it in his bedroom the day after his accident, got it working again with a new battery, and have barely taken it off since. Luckily, it fit me perfectly and did not require re-sizing. I love the fact that I can look down at my wrist and think of my little boy and how happy he was to receive his very first dress watch, wearing it on special occasions when he'd take off his everyday canvas band sports watch.

A few months after Steven's death, our family jeweler, Dave Kohler, made a very special gift for my daughters and me. He made us matching white gold heart charms. The face of the charm has a baseball bat with Steven's initials, "SBM," inscribed on it. Next to the bat is a diamond chip with the points of a star surrounding it. The charm, in essence, is Steven's baseball bat hitting a star in heaven. The girls and I absolutely loved and appreciated this gift, and I wear mine on a necklace every day. Francesca, Brianna and I make sure we wear ours together for special family pictures, knowing that it's our way of having Steven "in the photo" with us. Mine is getting a little tarnished from constantly rubbing the charm between my fingers and swinging it back and forth on the chain. Steven's charm brings peace to my day just by wearing it, and I'm so very thankful to our friend and jeweler for creating such a heartfelt symbol for us.

The girls and I wear our heart necklaces for family pictures.

About a year after Steven's death, I answered a knock at my front door. At my door were a few of Steven's good buddies, and I was delighted to see them. Just connecting with Steven's friends at any opportunity was such good, healing therapy for all of us. We enjoyed running into them around town, always sure to get a bright hello, a high five or hug.

I invited them in, and could tell they had a specific purpose for their unexpected visit. In their hands they held a small box, and on their faces were the looks of children who have something special to share. I was told that they had "made" something for me, and couldn't wait until Christmas to give it.

I opened the box, only to find the most precious gift from Bradley, Brett and Luke Bartuch, brothers and good friends of Steven's, their mom, Jill, close behind them with pride and emotion gleaming in her eyes, the same Jill who bakes us Steven's favorite chocolate chip cookies each year on his birthday. It was a very special charm bracelet, the type where the charms slide onto an elastic band, and all the charms depicted Steven in a huge way. There was a cross charm for his faith, a little dog depicting our Shih Tzu, "Scooby," his birthstone, a golf ball, baseball, basketball, and football honoring all the sports which Steven loved so much. There was even a chocolate chip cookie charm. There was a bicycle and a rainbow and a music note and Steven's favorite number "13." The best charm that the boys chose was one, which simply said, "Friends Forever." I wear the charm bracelet every day of my life. I twirl and twirl the charm bracelet around and see all of Steven's favorite things in life, any hour of any day, no matter where I am. Words cannot describe how much the bracelet means to me, and still does today as I wear it day after day, no matter what I have on, no matter where I'm going. I couldn't thank the boys enough for this enormously thoughtful gift, and think of them each time I look at the bracelet, reminding me of three special boys who are indeed Steven's friends *forever*.

The first year that my husband and I exchanged a true anniversary gift after we lost Steven, it was as though Steven himself, with his new divine intervention, had directed us to the perfect gift for each other.

I knew that my husband and family realized how much the angels and charms and all comforted me. I would dress every morning adorned in my little boy. I could touch my throat and feel the baseball charm, my wrist and feel his watch or the bracelet. I could be anywhere in my day and within a millisecond, feel my son's presence envelop me. These mementos helped me calm down when impending feelings of anxiety were ready to become full-blown attacks. So, on that first anniversary that we exchanged gifts, my husband Steve and I gave each other the gift of Steven, and in essence, of our "three" children.

To us, the symbol of the unity of our children being forever "three" are their initials together, "FSB," as in Francesca-Steven-Brianna. It means that nothing, not even death, can break their bond apart. They were three children born to us and they will forever be sister-brother-sister. I decided to get Steve a gift, which symbolized our "FSB" covenant, and chose a Tiffany's money clip with "FSB" engraved on it. He'd always liked to use money clips as opposed to wallets, and I felt sure that kids' initials on it would be very meaningful to him.

The morning of that wedding anniversary, June 27, 2005, will forever be etched in my mind. He did, indeed, love the money clip, especially because of the engraving. After he opened my gift, he stopped, shook his head and chuckled. He said, "I guess we really think alike more than we realize." As I opened mine, a small ring box, my heart sang. It was a simple white gold band, with the initials, FSB running a continuous circle around the band. It was symbolic of the unbroken chain of our kids as siblings, the unending circle of love now around my finger. I couldn't have loved any anniversary gift more, and enjoy wearing that band as I do all of the other daily symbols.

I am blessed to have good friends like a dear mom named Justine Santello who never forgets a graduation or milestone of Steven's, and always sends a small sentiment; an angel, a card, a Mass said in his name. We have family who remember occasions like Steven's sixteenth birthday when my siblings sent sixteen teddy bears to the young patients at Chicago's Children's Memorial Hospital in Steven's name. My friend Geri Galassini took a portion of Steven's school paper about remembering those we love in memory and keeping them alive for another day, had it reduced and enclosed it in a prayer box bracelet, and gave it to us on the night of what would have been Steven's Confirmation.

There are friends and family members who give up pop like Steven every year for Lent. There are neighbors who call to share a dream that had Steven in it and brought them comfort. Our little nephew, Nathan Malin, wrote a rainbow story for us. Our young family friend, Isabella Mancini, wrote an essay about Steven's baseball field being her favorite spot in town. There have been poems from Sally LaCrosse and songs from Peggy Schweller.

My sweet girlfriend, Raphaela and I met for shopping some months after losing Steven. She said she had a dream the night before where Steven told her to take me to the mall, that his mom always relaxed while browsing. She did the next day and we did relax.

My friend, Peggy, generously surprised me with two tickets for us to attend a presentation by James Van Praagh, the world-renowned medium, in the hopes that seeing this psychic, who helps those who've lost a loved one, would help me feel closer to Steven.

Indeed, those around us never stop bringing the light, always letting us know that we are not alone. Again, there are no words for these thought-filled gestures. If only they could see the lifelines they have given us when we thought we'd stay at the bottom of the ocean forever. They have helped raise us up, from those first moments to today. These unbelievable friends and family members do all they can to let us constantly know that "they remember," that they keep Steven close for us, with us. Indeed, we are the recipients of a wonderful family's kindnesses and a true community of givers, and we are the humble but grateful receivers.

* * *

CHAPTER 29: VIEWS FROM THE SAME CLIFF

So, when did it all begin to come together again? And is it ever permanently "together?" I guess the "together" quotient depends on the day. Some days are definitely more solid than others, and I think we finally forgive ourselves for a bad day, a bad week, knowing that we get through them all together. We'll always struggle more at milestones, birthdays, the holidays. I believe the key is that we get past these trying times; that we're committed to working toward the next "good" day, the next step in moving forward on the path, keeping Steven with us to help us fight the storms that still occasionally brew.

There's still no "normal" the way we once knew it and that, we know, will never return. We'll have normal days, normal outings, even "normal" conversations with good friends that include reflections on how "inconceivable" it is to them to fathom losing one of their own children. They fear it; they don't even want to think about it or verbalize it. "I can't even imagine" is what they say over and over to us. We always thought the death of one of our children was inconceivable, too. We felt like those tragedies happened to other people, but could never happen to folks as "normal" as us. We tell our friends that we pray every day that they never, ever experience this type of "inconceivable."

For the girls, I feel that time has allowed them to restructure their physical relationship from three to two, helping their dynamic, bringing them more full-circle. The inherent differences between a teenaged child and a middle school aged child naturally affect their communication and camaraderie, with or without a grief situation. Thankfully, I'm blessed to have girls who are good at releasing their feelings in a positive manner, of staying open, of being in touch with good and bad emotions. I also know that the more time that passes, the more they'll come together, much as the age gap closes as well. What's important to me is that they each talk to us, never afraid to lay the bad days out on the line along with the good ones, never hesitating to speak of their brother. This experience has stripped them of their innocence in many ways. They are strong young women who've seen too much pain in their tender lives, but I feel confident that their resiliency will benefit them immensely as adults and parents themselves.

I distinctly remember a picture from the first vacation we took as a family of four, a trip over three years after Steven went to heaven, to the Northern coast of California, that personally brought me more full circle as I watched a significant change in our girls' relationship. The genuine silly, sister-to-sister hamming-it-up-for-the-photo-op look on the girls' faces in this picture from a hotel in San Francisco spoke volumes to me as a mother about their progress in coming together again. Although I had feared the void of traveling as four, it had been three years, and we knew it was time to try to go somewhere without the buffer of another family along. We landed in LA, and spent a few days there as well as Santa Barbara, Carmel and San Francisco. As we drove from Santa Barbara to Carmel, I remember looking in the back seat of the rental car seeing a seventeen year-old and a twelve year-old passing time together doing nothing more than chatting and laughing as sisters, and simply watching the beautiful driving scenery of Pacific Coast Highway. It felt incredible to see them passing their time with each other like that. They sat "together" instead of sitting with the invisible gap of their middle brother between them. They took goofy pictures of each other with their digital cameras, oohed and aahed during the hairpin, cliff top turns of the drive on US-1, and generally did nothing more than be connected sisters passing the hours on a driving vacation. *And you were there with them in the photos and in the back seat of the car, Steven. We've kept your place with us, but just moved your sisters a little closer together.*

Francesca and Brianna in San Francisco, 2006.

I am still extremely overprotective of my girls, even more so than right after we lost Steven. As they've gotten older, they are naturally allowed to go more places, and I constantly fear how they travel to their destinations. I fear how Frankie gets to downtown Chicago to go shopping with her friends, where Bri walks while uptown Lake Forest for lunch with girlfriends. I'm not worried so much about the choices they make once they're at a destination as how they get to the destination itself. I irrationally fear the car that zooms up out of nowhere and hits them. I loathe the thought of them taking a train anywhere. I panic at letting them travel with another teen driver, or the sheer thought of driving to visit a friend at college. I am so, so lucky that, for the most part, my kids get my irrational fears and are so very, very patient with me. Like many parents, I must tell them I love them before they leave my sight. I know it would neither be possible nor logical to spend every waking minute with my kids. I must let them go to age-appropriate places without me, and live their lives with confidence. I cannot stifle their normal maturing process due to my irrational fears for their safety.

When I say good-night and they head to their beds, I still double kiss the air after I kiss my girls. I began a habit when my three kids were young of kissing them good-night in their beds then double-kissing the air as I closed their door. They'd double kiss back. It was our little way of saying, "I'll see you again." Smack-smack. Smack-smack. When I talk to Frankie at college and it's late at night, I'll end with, "Talk to you tomorrow, love you. Smack-smack." And she'll always double kiss back over the phone. To this day, I even quietly double-kiss the air when I leave Steven's bedroom at our house. When we all said good-bye to Steven for the last time before they closed his casket, I spontaneously told everyone they could double kiss the air as they saw him for the last time, a sure sign that they'd see Steven again and that this wasn't "good-bye." I still don't know why I did that. It was the last thing I should have been thinking about in that moment. But it was what first came to mind. More not wanting to say good-bye forever. Double kiss. See you again.

Moving to our new house has been a godsend as well as a challenge for us. Yes, it's provided a more peaceful locale away from the train horns. Yes, we hear distant horns that still affect my husband's sleep, but he's working so hard to overcome these fears. Brianna once told her dad to think of the train horns as "doing their job" to warn someone of the train's presence, that he should feel comfort that even though the horn wasn't able to save Steven, it is now keeping another person safe.

Our new house lacks the childhood memories our daughters so need to hang onto, yet has provided respite from being in a home that harbored much loneliness without Steven physically there. One of the challenges of our new house was to make it feel more like "home," because home to us means Steven's presence in it. One of the best parts of unpacking and setting up our new house was to bring back out our family pictures, especially those of the three kids when they were little. Galleries of photos grace this house, much like our other home. In fact, in keeping with my policy on equality as a mom, I even have an equal number of photos of each child hanging on each wall. Our "athletics" wall in the basement hosts thirty-nine portraits (lucky number "thirteen" for each child, naturally) of the kids in any number of past sports, from the first dance recitals to the high school cheerleading squads to the last baseball teams. Bringing the photos out definitely helped all of us feel like this was home again. We have dedicated spaces for Steven's childhood things, and his coats still hang in our closets. Where Steven is, this is "home" to us.

In the basement of our old house, we had a caricature drawn of our family of five on the wall of our exercise room. It became a bit of a group "self-portrait" so to speak, not to mention a great way to poke a little fun at ourselves. We were each featured in our favorite sports — tennis for me, golf for Steve, baseball for Steven, dance for Frankie and soccer for Bri. It killed me to leave that mural behind when we moved. So, I called the local artist, an extremely talented woman named Marilyn Adamovic, who originally drew it for us, and she was kind enough to duplicate the caricature on a canvas so we could take it along to the new house. She even generously made a gift of it for us.

A little over two years after Steven went to heaven, our family was hit with another tragic event, but one that ironically proved to provide me some long overdue closure to that fateful day in the hospital when Steven left us.

My mom, a sweet, gentle woman of seventy-nine years, came home from church on a Sunday morning in August of 2005, sat down at the kitchen table for coffee with my dad, and had a massive, hemorrhaging stroke. She hadn't been feeling well for about a year, unable to resolve a case of vertigo, which had come over her out of nowhere. My dad frantically called me up and said that my mom was fixed and unresponsive at the kitchen table. Living only three miles from my folks, I rushed over in my pajamas, calling 911 on my way so that the paramedics would reach my mom even before I did. Mom was rushed to the hospital and lay in the emergency room, her prognosis grim to say the least. Unbelievably, it was the very area of the ER where Steven was pronounced dead. Although my first thoughts were to do anything to help Mom, I was soon hit with a bolt in my stomach realizing that this was the area where Steven's room was. The room in which I begged God to spare my little boy. The room in which I begged God to take me instead. The room where I kissed his warm skin and soft cheeks for the very last time. Now the room where we were told my beloved mom would probably die her own death.

As my siblings and our spouses arrived one-by-one to join Dad and me, and I knew the situation was now in control by the rest of my family, I quietly left the room. The stabs in my stomach had overtaken me to such a degree that I could barely stand straight. I had also felt the symptoms of a bladder infection since the day before, and had been unable to get hold of my doctor that Saturday. Although I didn't feel well physically, the pains in my guts were not the infection, but surely the trauma of what I thought would be another loved one lost in that evil emergency room. Outside my mom's room, I sank to the ground against the wall in the corridor. My body wretched with convulsive tears as once again I didn't understand why I had been brought to this nightmarish place, how Mom could possibly die in the same place where Steven's life was taken away.

My brother, Gene, joined me and brought me to another quiet area where I could cry in peace. Again I was overcome with the "why's." *Why here? Why again? Why now Mom?* There was no logic, no connection, no reason why the nightmares always had to come back again. Gene listened patiently, his arm protectively around me yet again.

The hours of that sweltering August day ticked away, my mom being visited by any number of neurologists and neurosurgeons who all reiterated that her chances to survive were slim. She was finally moved up to Intensive Care late in the day, all of us following the slow journey out of the ER, my brother Gene offering to stay the night so she wouldn't be alone should she not make it through. We had all reached emotional exhaustion by that point, and the symptoms of my urinary tract infection had become extremely uncomfortable. My back throbbed, and later I'd learn that I had a kidney infection as well. My family insisted that I at least head back down to the emergency room and get tested and on an antibiotic. We all knew we'd go home for a few hours and be back early in the morning. Although everyone offered to come down with me, I decided to go down to the ER lab alone, even without Steve, and take advantage of a few minutes to gather my swirling thoughts and try to make sense of the events of the day. I knew I wouldn't be in that very room again, as the ER lab was in a separate area from where Mom and Steven were.

As I waited to be seen, a nurse entered to speak to me. She looked kindly and warm, and had a compassionate face and blond hair. I thought I'd never seen her before until I realized that indeed, I had. She was the very nurse who met Steve and I in the family room area to tell us of Steven's condition that fateful day. The very nurse who tried to tell us that Steven had not survived, and who I didn't want to listen to. I remembered her as being cold and unfeeling, wanting me to let go, not possibly being capable of knowing what my son's condition was or how to care for him or fix him. This day, she looked angelic as she reintroduced herself to me. She remembered me as well, had been on duty that whole Sunday, but didn't want to come in with my mom so ill and all of us there. I hugged her. We both cried quietly. She was real. She said she thought of us often.

The next person to come into the lab area and tell me the results of my tests was an older, portly, kind-faced doctor. He looked like a grandpa to me, caring and wise. Although he looked slightly familiar, I couldn't place him. He smiled at me and I crooked my head to try to remember how I knew him. He slowly shook his head, looked into my eyes, and said that he'd never forgotten my husband or me. It was the doctor who tried to save Steven that day. I only remembered a stern, unfeeling doctor who dared to tell me that my son had died. I hated that doctor. It couldn't be the gentle, grandfatherly man who now stood before me with tears in his eyes. *How could this be?* Why were this nurse and doctor there at this moment? Why did I really come down to the ER for the tests alone? I reached out my arms to this caring man and hugged him, crying my eyes out, releasing two and a half years of tears for these angels of mercy who, before this day, I believed wanted me to "let go." That night they hugged me and told me that they hang on to April 19, 2003. That they have never let us go in thought or heart. That they never forgot Steven or us. That they still pray for our family.

This night at the emergency room, reconnecting with these caring souls, I received the hugs of compassion that had to be held back that day as professionals facing a severe crisis must do. I was meant to see this doctor and nurse again because Steven and God knew that I needed to. I needed to see them as the gentle, wonderful people they were, and were that awful day, too. I still feel blessed that God and Steven brought them back to me. As I write this today, my mom is still physically "here," although the stroke has left her greatly incapacitated. She is still the gentle, sweet woman that she was that Sunday morning, and still Mom to me, much as Steven will always be one of my three children.

So, although cliffs remain to be jumped, we jump them without fear of someone truly being there to catch us on the other side. We've closed so many circles again; there are far fewer opportunities to fall into that black abyss. We are there for each other again. Home feels like home with family members who feel like family again. Steven's spiritual presence brings us symbols of closure, and we accept them with a circle of open arms.

* * *

CHAPTER 30: MOVING FORWARD, HANGING ON

I think back to life before Steven died. I often refer to it as "my old life." There is no doubt in my mind that I have lived two lifetimes, and they do not know each other. I try to remind myself that I have found happiness in both and even in this life, without my precious son, Maya Angelou reminds me that I am able to laugh as much as I cry.

Laugh? How are we allowed to laugh after a child dies? What does someone think when they see a mother whose lost a child laugh? Do they realize that she saves her tears for nighttime so as not to burden the daytime world with them? But I do laugh, and I don't cry myself to sleep nearly as often. Steven laughed, long and loud. Life is for laughter.

Dance? In this new life, surely I mustn't dance. How can you be a grieving mother who dances? A grieving mother only grieves, right? I feel as though I've slowly relearned to laugh and dance. For the first time, at a costume party four Halloweens after we lost Steven, a few of my closest girlfriends got me out on the dance floor, all of us in ridiculous costumes, and I danced. Not just the requisite one slow dance with my husband at the few weddings we've been to these past years. A real, goofy, kickline-with-your-girlfriends dance. And it made me feel so alive. I laugh. I dance. I grieve. I live.

Steven still visits my dreams, but now they're happy visitations. Sometimes I am merely buying him his North Face jacket for the fall season. Other times he's just there, right where he belongs, with the girls and us. I continue to parent him in my world of dreams and sleep, but there are no more nightmares. I have finally said "good-bye" and good riddance to those. No more cold death; no more hail-pummeling hell. Only life; only good. Steven with us. Right where he'll always belong.

When I look back at my old life, I feel as though I'm looking into the window of a store, and I'm on the outside looking in. Through the glass, I see a young mom with three small children — one holding her hand, one in the stroller, one hanging onto the stroller. The mom looks busy but happy. The kids are safe. The life is secure and the routine predictable. The four of them spend their predictably simple days together. This woman has it all — a good husband, these three God-given children, two loving parents, family and friends who surround her with a lot of happiness. I tap on the glass but no one turns around to acknowledge me. I call out to get the woman's attention, and with no response, simply continue to watch this other person's life. The steam from my breath accumulates on the glass as I whisper, "Turn around. Let me see what heaven looks like." I want to tell this woman that I'd give anything to be her. But then I realize — I *was* her.

I know I look at that life as more idyllic than it really was because it's the life I still want back with every fiber of my being. Life hasn't ever or shouldn't ever be perfect, but I look back now and see that having the five of us all together made it perfect. It was all that truly mattered. I felt whole. Life was whole. That meant everything to me. Still, I move forward, and I must take each new step with complete, whole effort.

I thank God every day for my two beautifully strong, articulate daughters. I am still filled with daily gratitude for the gifts of these precious girls who keep me focused on living; their accomplishments, their goals keep me alive with life. They even tell me that they'll each have more children so I still someday have the crowd of grandchildren I have always wished for. I am so blessed to be Frankie and Bri's mom, to be here, whole, physically, mentally and emotionally to give them everything they need from me. I truly hope that I have come out of this a better listener for them. I know that I'm still a stubborn Italian mom who wants to be heard loud and clear on the teenage issues and messages. But with the deep feelings, the communication of our hearts, I pray that they know I now listen with more openness and receiving than I ever had before.

I pray that I still count my blessings enough. I praise God every day and thank Him. I trust in the path He has chosen, although I'll never understand it on this earth. I count Steven among my blessings every day, although he isn't physically here. I have passed the crossroads and reached another side, something I wasn't sure I ever could do. And I've done it because I've kept Steven with me in heart, word and deed. The affirmations of his continued existence in our lives, the signs, are blessings to be thankful for. And I still think of heaven. But the heaven I now envision isn't my life here on this earth, or my old life as viewed through a glass pane. It's when the five of us are reunited up there. The big heaven. The real deal. The blessing of all blessings. The whole that can never be broken again.

Then I think of the "me" now. I am full of texture, enriched, a wiser, deeper thinker than I ever wanted to be. But who wants to be wise for this reason? I am still down deep, *me*, only changed. I see clarity in situations where before I was part of the "haze." I get angered when I hear other parents complain about their kid having a bad game or not getting an "A." What I wouldn't give for a lifetime without an "A" on Steven's report card, as long as he had a lifetime to live.

I bet it's hard to be friends with me now. I don't want to be treated differently, but I *am* different. I look at life's experiences so honestly, too honestly now, and find little patience for superficiality, pretense, and those who don't live authentically, who are just content to live in the shallow end of the pool. So many times I want to scream, "Come talk to me when your child is dead in your arms," but surely I cannot. I can't inflict what's happened to me into everything in this new life. It isn't fair to those around me, and it's not how I consciously want to live. It's only my scab falling off now and again, my wounds reopening. I try to make concerted efforts to honor the grief of others — a parent or grandparent who's died — and tell others that I can't imagine how they feel. The truth is that I really can't. Just as no one can know my pain, I can't know others', and it's so important to take steps back to honor and respect the depth of someone else's grief feelings.

I feel such extreme gut instincts about things now, and I find it hard not to act on them when I am so overwhelmed with some greater force pushing me along, knowing that it's Steven. It was hard to say "no" to him in my old life, and still hard now, I guess. I feel a greater force to do good for others. Maybe this is only because I realize how precious life is, and how it's so important to have the good always outweigh the bad.

I know that time will never change me back to who I was before Steven went to heaven. I am forever a changed Maria in a new life on this earth. As I've said, there's no going back to the old life. If you have buried a child, that sweet, precious existence you once knew is nothing but a sweet, precious memory. You can remember your old life, but there's no use trying to maintain the old "you's." They died along with your child. Yes, I will always have three children; I will always be Steven's mother. And here, while still tending to this new life, I must always preserve our morals, values and life messages, which must never change.

I have always been a mom who wanted her children to look for the winter wonderlands after the snowfalls. When the kids were little, we'd drive around and "ooh" and "ahh" at nature's beauty. We'd go looking for the field of sunflowers that wasn't to be missed. We'd watch a magical red sunset over the trees where we live and chant, "Red sky at night, sailor's delight. Red sky at morn, sailors be warned" and laugh at the unison, quietly marveling at nature's beauties. We looked for signs in that life, and we'll always look now. This simply cannot go away. I want my daughters to take their small children to look at the city of Chicago from a Ferris wheel, no matter if it's scary from so high. To sit in the backyard at dusk and chant about the color of the sky. To see the wonderlands created when the snow is wet and the morning silent. To look for signs from heaven. To hold life's precious truths and morals as templates for how we are to live our lives.

Yes, I will forever grieve. No, I am not depressed. I realize now what a big difference there is between the two, and it's taken me so long to get here. This is why it's okay to laugh *and* to dance and cry, too. You can laugh and dance and grieve, but it's hard to even want to live while depressed. To me, grief is a feeling. Depression is a state. That day at the train crossing, I chose to live. I will live with grief, but I will live.

Tragedies make us close ourselves up and form a protective barrier toward another hurt or pain. We live smaller, safer, not meeting anyone new, thinking we're sheltering ourselves from another disaster. But living in this fear isn't really living. We were initially in a cocoon, hiding from more pain, more loss, not being able to take one more iota of stress from any source. This isn't normal life, but I wondered what would ever constitute some degree of "normalcy" again.

It's taken these years to realize that "normal" includes daily stresses, daily blessings, traffic jams and a few bad hair days. And being okay with acknowledging all of them. It's okay to sweat the small stuff sometimes because that's what "normal" daily life is. Because we've been enlightened to what's truly important in life, of course these small things don't carry nearly the weight that they did before. When we first lost Steven, everything was put on a playing field comparing "this or that" in life to losing Steven. Obviously, nothing compares, and we can't go on living in comparison of the worst thing that's ever happened to us. Traffic is traffic. Bad hair days are bad hair days. It's okay to live them, deal with small stresses, and bless the good each and every day. It's life again.

So, have we "defeated" death? No. No one wins that big. Death will knock at the door, but we will never again answer the door in the same way. We will never let death take our loved one away again. We will keep them forever close. We'll look for the signs, the symbols, keeping their name on our lips every day, feeling their inspiration push us along, feeling their protection over our shoulder. Death will never again strip us of these.

The pendulum of sadness still swings, and always will. The momentum, the arc of the swing is just less. The bad is not as bad; the good is recognized. We function, good or bad day. Alan tells me that it's okay to allow a downward spiral of emotions, as long as I rise again and keep moving forward. Bad days bring me forward to a good day.

So again, I challenge you to not accept the biggest "no" of your life. Say "yes" to hanging on, to keeping your loved one with you. It is not enough to survive — I know I had to choose to live, and live with Steven close to me forever. Steven is still with me, and with every breath I take, and your child or loved one can be, too. When I made the conscious decision not to end my own life, I also made a decision to live, from that day forward, with my son firmly embedded in every step of every day until I see him again. Is this what "full circle" means? I don't honestly know. I'd like to think that I have simply not allowed our circle to open enough to let one of us out permanently.

So, I urge you not to let go. Yes, move forward. Yes, live life for the rest of your family. Yes, continue to embrace your child in thought, memory and deed. You will not be sorry that you *just could not say good-bye.*

On our plane trip home from that special vacation to Florida, two weeks to the day when our son and brother would be taken to heaven, I sat next to Steven, he at the window seat and me in the middle, and together, we worked on a paper that was due when he returned from spring break. The topic was "heroes," and Steven wrote with an insight he certainly had no conscious knowledge of. The heroes he spoke of would be the very same that would try in vain to save his life just fourteen days later — the paramedics, firemen, doctors, nurses who all worked with heroic effort to bring life back into Steven's lifeless body. He wrote:

> *We think of heroes in many ways. Heroes could be policemen, firefighters, a sports figure, or even a dog that rescues someone out of danger. Heroes have many qualities that set them apart from others. Three of these qualities are courage, leadership, and self-confidence.*

Heroes display much courage in their actions. Heroes are willing to take risks to get the job done. They are willing to take the harder route on a long journey. Also, they don't give up until their end result is achieved. To them, their own safety is not as important as a normal person. Indeed, they display courage to protect others from danger. They put others before themselves. They are even willing to sacrifice their own safety when rescuing people from danger. As a result, they live to help others.

Heroes are leaders because of the good example they set for others. In fact, heroes are great role models. Likewise, others hope to live their life the way heroes do. They influence the best and most that someone can be. We look up to heroes because of the example they set. Also, heroes have strong leadership characteristics. They guide others to achieve their desired goals. Similarly, they help others strive for higher results. All of this makes people feel safe under the guidance of a hero.

Heroes use self-confidence to believe in themselves and their abilities. They stay focused in their actions. In addition, they have good concentration and plan well. For example, they don't let other things come before their good deeds. They are usually highly trained in their profession. Also, they are confident that they will achieve their goal. They inspire others to believe in them. They think positive instead of negative about things. Last, they do not get discouraged by their obstacles.

> *These three qualities (there are many more) are what make a hero someone that is looked up to. These three qualities are courage, leadership, and self-confidence. These qualities show their strength, determination, and motivation for the successful result no matter what the price. In conclusion to all of this, I have to say thank goodness for heroes because their lives make such a good impression of all of the lives that they touch. Our world is a better place with heroes.*

After Steven finished the draft of the paper, he and I relaxed for the remainder of the flight home. He ordered a lemonade, and we sat and talked about nothing and everything, which we often did. At one point, we were flying above an especially fluffy cluster of clouds, and Steven looked over at me. It was characteristically like him or the girls to notice something as simple as the beauty of cloud formations out an airplane window. And with a serene smile, that ever-swirled front cowlick, and those soft, soft brown eyes fringed by long black lashes, he slowly turned to me and said, "Kind of looks like heaven, doesn't it, Mom?"

* * *

Contact Maria Malin at www.movingforwardhangingon.com.

"Our family is a circle of love,
our friends are a circle of strength,
our future is a circle of hope,
our faith is a circle of peace."

Maria Malin, 2004

Made in the USA